MULTIPLYING
CHURCHES
IN JAPANESE SOIL

[handwritten inscription]

To Amy &
Thank you for
the commitment
to multiplying churches.

Mt 16:18

John Mehn

I've known John for more than a decade and am thankful for his faithful gospel work in Japan. Now, I'm thrilled that many others can be encouraged and better equipped for church planting in Japan via his writing.

Ed Stetzer, PhD
Billy Graham Distinguished Chair
of Church, Mission, and Evangelism,
Wheaton College

Japan is known as one of the most resistant nations to the advance of the gospel. And yet some Japanese churches are remarkably effective in planting new churches and reproducing fruitful ministries. What are these churches doing and what are the qualities of the leaders in these movements? John Mehn's research discovers answers to these questions against the backdrop of the historic and current state of Christianity in Japan and by exploring various ministry models. *Multiplying Churches in Japanese Soil* is a welcome and important addition to our understanding of mission and church planting, offering insights that will be helpful and encouraging to Christian leaders everywhere.

Craig Ott, PhD
professor of mission and intercultural studies
Trinity Evangelical Divinity School

John Mehn offers us here a unique contribution. This book combines various approaches that are often kept separate because of their individual challenges. Mehn's approach is contemporary while drawing on historical trends and examples. This work is practical while drawing on biblical, theological, and principled discussions. Lessons from a wide spectrum of traditions—including Orthodox and Holiness, for example—feed a distinctively evangelical fervor for church growth. The result is a passionate, encouraging, and faith-filled vision for how healthy churches can multiply in Japan like never before.

J. Nelson Jennings, PhD
mission pastor and consultant, Onnuri Community Church, Seoul
former missionary to Japan

Japan has long been an enigma to missiologists. Despite centuries of Christian presence in Japan, Christians remain a tiny minority in a highly modernized—but also highly traditional—society. In this informative work, veteran missionary church planter John Mehn provides a helpful overview of Christianity in Japan today and suggests some very practical ways in which Christians can meet current challenges and opportunities, resulting in a new era of church multiplication.

Harold Netland, PhD
professor of philosophy of religion and intercultural studies,
Trinity Evangelical Divinity School
former missionary to Japan

John Mehn has presented a comprehensive overview of important issues involved in church growth and multiplication in Japan. The final chapters are particularly helpful in showing some of the features that facilitate these processes today. Besides stimulating prayer for the Japanese people, I hope that this book will encourage many ministering among the Japanese to apply these practical insights in their local contexts.

David C. Lewis, PhD
fellow of the Royal Anthropological Institute
author of *The Unseen Face of Japan*

The gospel has been in Japan for centuries, yet the Japanese remain one of the world's largest unreached people groups. John Mehn has written an honorable work that examines Japan's past and present realities that our Sovereign Lord is working through to build his church. This book is an important contribution to missiological studies and filled with principles and practical guidance based on field research. With over thirty years of service in Japan, Mehn writes with both a scholar's mind and servant's heart, and offers hope for the multiplication of disciples, leaders, and churches among this great people.

J. D. Payne, PhD
pastor of church multiplication, The Church at Brook Hills
author of *Apostolic Church Planting*

MULTIPLYING
CHURCHES
IN JAPANESE SOIL

JOHN WM. MEHN

WILLIAM CAREY
LIBRARY

Published by William Carey Library
1605 E. Elizabeth St.
Pasadena, CA 91104 | www.missionbooks.org

Melissa Hughes, editor
Joanne Liang, graphic design

William Carey Library is a ministry of
Frontier Ventures
www.frontierventures.org

Printed in the United States of America
21 20 19 18 17   5 4 3 2 1 BP

Library of Congress Cataloging-in-Publication Data
Names: Mehn, John Wm., author.
Title: Multiplying churches in Japanese soil / John Wm. Mehn.
Description: Pasadena, CA : William Carey Library, 2017. | Includes
  bibliographical references and index. |
Identifiers: LCCN 2017040688 (print) | LCCN 2017041149 (ebook) | ISBN
  9780878088508 (eBook) | ISBN 9780878085446 (pbk.) | ISBN 0878085440 (pbk.)
Subjects: LCSH: Christianity--Japan. | Japan--Church history. | Church
  development, New--Japan. | Church growth--Japan. | Missions--Japan. |
  Evangelistic work--Japan.
Classification: LCC BR1305.5 (ebook) | LCC BR1305.5 .M44 2017 (print) | DDC
  266.00952--dc23
LC record available at https://lccn.loc.gov/2017040688

CONTENTS

ILLUSTRATIONS

FIGURES

TABLES

LIST OF ABBREVIATIONS

CIS	Church Information Service, Japan
CPI	Church Planting Institute
CPM	Church Planting Movement
CRASH Japan	Christian Relief, Assistance, Support, and Hope
DAWN	Discipling A Whole Nation
DRC-Net	Disaster Relief Coordination Network
GCPN	Global Church Planting Network
JCE6	Japan Sixth Congress on Evangelism
JCGI	Japan Church Growth Institute (currently the JCGI Network)
JCMN	Japan Cell Church Mission Network
JEA	Japan Evangelical Association [Nihon Fukuin Dōmei]
JEMA	Japan Evangelical Missionary Association
JMR	Japan Mission Research
KDK	Kokunai Dendō Kai [National Evangelism Association]
Kyōdan	Nihon Kirisuto Kyōdan [United Church of Christ in Japan]
MMN	Miyagi Mission Network
NCD	Natural Church Development
PDC	Purpose Driven Church
RJCPN	Rural Japan Church Planting Network

ACKNOWLEDGMENTS

This book is the product of many ministry experiences, personal discussions, and training situations in the trenches of church planting in Japan. Thanks to all who have made that journey with me. I am indebted to those I have partnered with in the Japan Baptist Church Association (Rengo), Church Information Service (CIS), and the Japan Evangelical Missionary Association. During this time, I have benefited by many coaches and mentors, notably Steve Childers, Stu Batstone, and Craig Ott.

To you who have in faith attempted to plant multiplying churches in Japan, I salute you. The Church Planting Institute (CPI) movement and community has been a hotbed for the content of this book. Thanks to those who have served on the CPI Leadership Team for their impact on my vision, heart, leadership, and ministry. These include Seima Aoyagi, Gary Fujino, Jay Greer, Pat Hansen, Dan Iverson, Akira Mori, Andy Rodriguez, Seita Sakaguchi, Jeremy Sink, Dave Walker, Charlie Williams, and Bruce Young.

Many Japanese leaders were my encouragers, and particularly regarding writing this book, namely Jiro Chida, Makoto Fukuda, Mitsuo Fukuda, Yoshiya Hari, Yukio Hanazono, Hiroshi Kawasaki, Hideo Ohashi, Takeshi Takezawa, and Shigeru Tsukura. Also, I want to recognize the Church Multiplication Vision Festa leaders and the JCE6 Church Multiplication Team.

Many friends and colleagues agreed to review my draft manuscript and shared their insights, reflections, and comments, including Laurence Hiebert, John Houlette, Patric Knaak, David Lewis,

Don Schaeffer, Rick Shenk, Nathan Snow, Carlton Walker, and Pastor Nobuo Watanabe.

Most of all I owe a great debt to my dear wife Elaine for her encouragement, patience, and practical help. Thank you, Tim and Beth, for journeying with me as we pursued God's call on our lives.

Special acknowledgment to William Carey Library for their frontier mission vision and hands-on work that the gospel may be shared in all the nations and especially to Joelle Bridges for her passion for Japan and dedication and skill for this project.

Figure 1. Map of Japan

INTRODUCTION

This book is about new churches in Japan. Why are many new churches needed, why we do not yet have them, and how we can work together for God's glory to see them planted in Japanese soil?

QUESTIONS

Often in discussing the cause of Christ's gospel in Japan—whether in regard to the church or missions—we hear the same questions. Why are there so few believers and such small churches in Japan? Is the church growing in Japan? Compared to other countries why does Japan seem so unresponsive to Christ?

These questions arise against the backdrop of one of the most accessible mission fields in the world, which has received sizable numbers of missionaries especially since World War II. These questions resonate with those who have served in Japan, for many who have a burden to see the Great Commission fulfilled among the Japanese, and those who long for Japan to become a mobilized missionary sending nation.

REALITY

Those are great questions when faced with the stark reality of the progress of Christianity in Japan. The country of Japan has the tenth largest population in the world with 127 million people; however, the percentage of Christians in Japan is miniscule: under 1 percent. The Japanese are truly in need as the second largest unreached people group in the world (Joshua Project 2015).

Japan is admired and emulated worldwide. Just 150 years ago, Japan emerged from medieval feudalism to become a modernized world-class nation. In more recent years, many have seen Japan rise to be a major industrialized power and a leader in Asia, now the third largest global economy. The Japanese people today are literate, educated, highly skilled, hardworking, and productive. Japan's society is stable, relatively crime-free, technologically advanced, and cutting-edge modern. Often world news on economics, politics, science, pop culture, or tourism in Japan are reported. In 2011 Japan garnered unusual global attention after the triple disaster of the earthquake, tsunami, and Fukushima nuclear accident.

Historically we have seen Japan progress as a nation but not the commensurate progress of the gospel among the Japanese. The entire country contains about eight thousand churches, and today many cities and towns still lack local churches.

Probably not as well-known is the history of Christianity in Japan over this same period, which is an amazing story of Christian sacrifice and perseverance. After first being introduced[1] in Japan by Catholic missionaries like Francis Xavier in 1549, Christianity grew rapidly to over 300,000 believers[2], which is a higher percentage of Christians than today (Mullins 2006, 116). This period of tremendous reception has been called "the Christian Century." Then, as the result of several factors, the government of Japan outlawed Christianity entirely with several edicts. Japanese believers then suffered the most systematic persecution and elimination of Christians in history (Earhart 2014, 168).

---

1. Some advocate that the first Christians in Japan were from the Church of the East (identified by others as the Nestorians) traveling through China beginning in the fifth century. There is strong evidence of these missionary efforts throughout China from the third century. Though intriguing, the historical evidence for their number in Japan is highly circumstantial and not compelling.

2. This is a conservative number. Some estimate there may have been as many as 760,000 believers.

Christians were eradicated from Japan except for a very small group of *kakure kirishitan* or "hidden Christians." Then Japan retreated behind a wall of isolation from the rest of the world for nearly 250 years.

In 1854, Japan was forced open by Western powers and Christianity returned. The Catholic missionary efforts returned and for the first time Protestants missionaries entered Japan. Once the official edict against Christianity was reversed in 1873, the number of Christians rapidly grew (Mullins 2006, 117). Church growth nearly halted when the Imperial Rescript on Education enforced in 1890 reinforced the role of the Japanese Emperor in national life. The years leading up to World War II saw a rise in State-sponsored Shrine Shintoism, and the church underwent a period of strict control followed by overt persecution. The post-war Japanese constitution affirmed separation of religion and State, so with these new freedoms, Christianity grew once again. The church in Japan has been a story of perseverance countering government restriction and the persecution that curbed the growth of the church. This exemplary perseverance of the Japanese church is a model for the church around the world.

For its relatively small size, the influence of Christianity in Japanese society has been extraordinary. This influence grows from significant historical leaders and academic institutions that were started during "the Christian Century" and the Meiji period (1868–1912). Today Christian education is widespread from kindergarten through grade school, junior, and senior high, to include some of the most prestigious universities in Japan. Other influences include medicine, labor unions, social reform movements, and politics (Mullins 2006, 120). Japan is the beneficiary of significant Christian resources such as Bibles, literature and publishing, media ministries, and theological seminaries and Bible schools. Japan, comparatively speaking, already has a high per capita number of missionaries serving overseas. Japan with its strength economically, educationally, and technologically has high potential for impact in world missions, as Japanese can go some places many others cannot.

So, despite its exemplary development as a nation, the Japanese are the epitome of a people unresponsive to the gospel. Japan presents many formidable cultural, historical, sociological, and spiritual challenges for evangelism, church planting, and growing and multiplying the Christian church.

THE TASK

God has a mission for Japan and the world. The triune God of the Bible is a missionary God, and God's intention is to draw worshippers for himself from every unreached kingdom and tribe and people. This fulfillment is recorded by John in the book of Revelation. "After this I looked and there before me was a great multitude that no one could count, from every nation, tribe, people and language, standing before the throne and in front of the Lamb. They were wearing white robes and they were holding palm branches in their hands. And they cried out in a loud voice: 'salvation belongs to our God, who sits on the throne, and to the Lamb'" (Rev 7:9–10; cf. 5:9–10). That scene will no doubt include Japanese worshippers.

This missionary intention of God is recorded throughout the Bible. Jesus after his resurrection gave repeated instructions for the disciples about this global task. The Great Commission to his disciples was the clear mandate to "make disciples of all nations" (Matt 28:19). The means of evangelism and the multiplication of disciples is accomplished through the church, since the church is central to the mission of God (Peters 1981, 20). Christ promised, "I will build my church, and the gates of Hades will not overcome it" (Matt 16:18). Christ established his church to fulfill the mission of God; consequently, the church possesses God's missionary nature. This missionary nature of the church needs deeper exploration in Japan to produce a renewed missionary understanding of the church and to practically carry on God's mission.

The "church as community of the kingdom is both the primary agent as well as the chief fruit of the *missio Dei* [mission of God] in this age" (Ott and Strauss 2010, vii). Since the primary task of God's mission is the church, the establishment of new churches is critical to fulfilling that mission. "The biblical record leaves no mistake that church planting is essential to God's salvation purposes and the fulfillment of the Great Commission" (Ott & Wilson 2011, 20).[3] The multiplication of new churches was the pattern seen in the book of Acts and notably practiced by the Apostle Paul who planted, multiplied, and facilitated the establishment of new churches (O'Brien 1995; Stetzer 2012). Moreover, throughout the progress of missions around the world, establishing new churches has been proven the best way to evangelize and disciple any people group. This also has been evidenced in the periods of growth of the church in Japan. In various settings, as God's sent people proclaimed the good news, those who responded in faith were formed into indigenous kingdom communities. Those churches in turn sent more into harvest ministry.

"The essential missionary task is to establish a viable indigenous church planting movement" (Winter and Koch 1999, 517) among every people group. The Japanese, who are less than one percent Christian, are an unreached people group necessitating missionary assistance in establishing and growing the church. Viewing the matter practically, about eight thousand churches and one million believers seem insufficient on their own to effectively proclaim the gospel in all areas of Japan. Japan needs many more churches, especially in unchurched areas. Only multiplying new communities of believers saturating the country will

---

3. For a fuller treatment on the theology of mission and church planting, please see Ott and Wilson 2011, 3–61.

accomplish that strategic task of displaying the missionary nature of the church in every community.

> Church planting initiatives are needed which are motivated by the privilege of participating in the mission of God [*missio Dei*], which are patterned on the incarnational way in which God has acted in mission, and which are energized by a vision of the coming kingdom of God as the goal of this mission. (Murray 2001, 52–53)[4]

Until an indigenous redemptive community (church) penetrates every nook and cranny of Japan, the biblical task in mission will not be completed. These dynamic, growing, and sending communities accomplish mission by sharing the gospel of the kingdom of God in word and deed towards the transformation of individuals and society. Furthermore, this biblical vision of God is not merely to reach Japan with the gospel but to see the vision fulfilled of reaching all of the nations for his glory.

OPPORTUNITY

In the midst of the current situation and many formidable challenges in Japan, greater prospects exist for multiplying new churches among the Japanese. For Japan, often considered a difficult culture, promising reports coming from the frontlines are bringing new hope. Current field research and trends on the ground indicate greater potential for church multiplication. Many are encouraged that ministry innovation engaging Japanese culture over the last several decades has been bearing fruit, which will be developed throughout the book.

Since the Japanese church exists, opportunity also still exists, because God is real and brings hope. God has sustained his

---

4. For more on the relationship between the church and the kingdom of God, see Allison 2012, 89–100.

church in Japan; it has persevered and is an indigenous base for more church planting. To build the church (1 Cor 3:10–15) the Japanese soil has been cultivated and watered, weeded and fertilized over many years by so many united "fellow workers" such as dedicated pastors, missionaries, and church members. And God has given growth to the Japanese church (1 Cor 3:5–9). There are hundreds of thousands of Christians in Japan waiting with patience, praying with expectation, and trusting in the hope of a greater breakthrough from God.

But some believe there is now great potential for church multiplication. Various social changes in Japan have impacted the responsiveness to Christianity. Not unlike the social changes in the "Christian Century," the Meiji restoration, and post-World War II, Japan has recently undergone significant social change. After the burst of the bubble economy in 1989, Japan went through "the lost decade" of repeated recessions changing the economy, employment, and bringing about the decline of the *kaisha* (the company) system with its dominance over adult life. These changes of social structure, marriage, and the general face of Japan have led to feelings of dissatisfaction and unrest (Matsumoto 2002, 28). The young people who lived through the nineties have been labeled the "lost generation" (Zielenziger 2006); characterized by depression, social withdrawal, escapism, and lack of opportunity, they now embrace values divergent from cultural tradition. The Great Hanshin earthquake in 1995 also forced changes in the church and society. The nerve gas attack by the new religion Aum Shinrikyo in 1995 shook up society in various ways by casting doubts and has stiffened Japanese resistance to religion, especially to organized groups like Aum Shinrikyo, which has been labeled a "pariah organization" (Earhart 2013, 235). The domination of the organized religions of Shintoism and Buddhism in Japan has gradually diminished due to increasing mobility and changes in family makeup resulting from urbanization and industrialization.

Still, spiritual challenges remain because of Japan's new religions and the continuing beliefs and practices of folk religion.

From this changing environment, the church responded admirably after the Great Tohoku Disaster in 2011 with great compassion and ministry. God used the disaster to raise up a new generation of ministry leaders (Hari 2017, 57–58). Walls fell between individual churches and denominations, resulting in more unity and cooperation. Walls also fell between the churches and their communities. Churches have been active by sharing and demonstrating hope to the Japanese and many believe there has never been a better time than now. Because of evangelism and church planting efforts, some prefectures in the Tokoku region have seen upwards of a 300 percent increase in churches.

People from all over the globe have been aware of the spiritual lostness of Japan, and they have been praying for God to be merciful and for a spiritual breakthrough. Even Christians in countries with historically tense relationships with Japan due to the horrors of World War II—namely Korea, China, Singapore, and the Philippines—have been praying fervently for Japan. Since the 2011 disaster this interest and prayer has increased.

Already some churches are reproducing in Japan, probably more than most people realize. But what is truly encouraging is the growing vision for church multiplication in Japan. In the past, some visionary leaders have bravely promoted doubling the number of churches (Kishida 1992). Today's Japanese leaders are not merely talking about doubling the existing churches but discussing multiplying churches to ten thousand, twenty thousand, even fifty thousand new churches for Japan! These numbers of churches are greater than any historical number of churches in Japan. Equally radical are the types of churches that these leaders are envisioning.

NEW QUESTIONS

Leaders stand in the gap between our current reality and our God-given visions and dreams. This leads us to ask big questions about our ministry. The new questions being asked are:

- Where is God working in Japan? Where is the wind of the Spirit blowing?
- Where can we learn how to do ministry better? Where are the effective model churches?
- How can we revisit and rediscover the real strengths of the Japanese church?
- What is needed to bring revival and reformation to the existing church?
- What are the most effective means of evangelizing and discipling Japanese?
- How does Christian community actively demonstrate the gospel of grace, forgiveness, acceptance, and freedom for Japanese scarred by society and without hope?
- How can more Christians engage with their neighbors, classmates, fellow workers, friends, and relatives in a vibrant experiential expression of Christianity?
- What churches are reproducing and multiplying churches? What is working in actual practice?
- How are churches multiplying disciples and developing leadership?
- What kind of leadership is reproducing churches in Japan?
- How are lay people being mobilized to plant churches?
- How can the church penetrate Japanese culture causing the roots of the gospel to flourish in the soil of Japan?

TOPICS

We will honestly take a hard look at the condition of the church in Japan while at the same time seeking new and fresh vision from God. Principles and practical guidance will be presented from ground-breaking field research. This book grows out of actual training courses and materials used in practical church planting training. Though not a church planter's manual, this will give guidance to church planters and strategists on ministry models and leadership roles and style. Through many case studies and best practices, those burdened for church multiplication on Japanese soil will gain new hope.

This book is not about theoretical visions and dreams but about visions and dreams concretely realized. It is a new call to prayer and a call to use God's spiritual resources to face the challenges of Japanese culture with a new vigor towards an unprecedented wave in the number of churches. Fresh insights and ideas for innovative ministry will be presented that will stimulate readers' thinking in new avenues and incite exploration of different paradigms.

The following chapters will include lessons, opportunities, potential, and possibilities to thrive in ministry and to combat the *status quo*. Through these chapters, the hope is for the reader to learn and experiment with some ministry innovations gleaned from history, to experience a shift of paradigms, and to strive ahead with new approaches and models. The end goal is to emulate those effective leaders and mobilize more for church planting. By means of case studies and research, the following topics will be explored in subsequent chapters.

Chapter One: Gospel Penetration in Japanese Soil. An external look at the progress of the gospel in Japan. What are the main reasons for the lack of response?

Chapter Two: The Church in Japanese Soil. An internal look at the state of the church in Japan. What is the health and relevance of the Japanese church?

Chapter Three: Japanese Religious Movements. What were some growing church movements? And what lessons can be learned from some Japanese social and religious movements?

Chapter Four: Strategic Perspectives on Church Planting. For the establishment of churches and movements in Japan what strategic principles were applied in history? What are some current trends?

Chapter Five: Effective Models of Reproducing Churches in Japan. What church models are effectively reproducing churches? How can we apply principles from these models for more effectiveness?

Chapter Six: Leaders Reproducing Churches. What can Japanese leaders who are effectively reproducing churches teach us about leadership?

Chapter Seven: Future Challenges for Multiplying New Churches. What should be done to assure church multiplication in Japanese soil?

We have briefly surveyed Japan considering God's task of establishing new churches. Next, we will pursue more deeply these challenging questions in examining the penetration of the gospel in the soil of Japan.

GOSPEL PENETRATION
IN JAPANESE SOIL

The Japanese soil has been a great challenge for the gospel, yet the gospel endures in Japan. The good news of God's reconciliation with man has resulted in many Japanese becoming children of God. And the church, the body of Christ, exists among the Japanese. The impact of a small number of Japanese believers is far greater than any collected statistics on the size of the church. However, as shared in the Introduction, the penetration and growth of the gospel in the soil of Japan has been meager and slow-paced.

We have considered some questions and opportunities in the task of advancing the Christian gospel in Japan. Now we turn to the response of the Japanese to the gospel. First, we will take a comprehensive look at the current situation in Japan. This hard look may seem difficult, but this baseline information will further instruct us as we consider ministry innovations from practical case studies. Then we will consider major reasons for the lack of response in Japan followed by some practical ways to address these hindrances.

GOSPEL PENETRATION IN JAPAN

Japan has a small percentage of Christians and Christian activity. Of the 126.9 million people of Japan, current membership of all Christian churches in Japan totals 1,065,049 [617,056 Protestants, 437,742 Catholics, and 10,251 Orthodox] (see Table 1) putting the total percentage of all Christians in Japan at 0.84 percent (JCE6 2016, 11). A reliable barometer of spiritual activity is weekly church attendance, and on any given Sunday about

280,000 Japanese are in a Protestant church service, which is about 0.22 percent of the population (CIS 2013, 5). Makito Goto believes these percentages are inflated reports and probably in reality much lower (Goto 2011, 15).

Table 1. Japan Churches and Membership

	Number of Churches	Total Membership
Catholic	1,000	437,742
Orthodox	70	10,251
Protestant	7,969	617.056
TOTAL	9,039	1,065,049

Source: (JCE6 2016, 11)

Japan contains one of the most homogeneous people groups on the planet. With a large middle-class they are culturally and ethnically similar. This large people group is the second largest unreached people group in the world (Joshua Project 2015). Besides the Japanese, other people groups are present in Japan; however, they are very small including the *Ainu* (an indigenous group), the *Burakumin* (the outcasts), and several ethnic groups on the Ryukyu Islands (Okinawa). Japan also has large numbers of Chinese (665,847) and Koreans (457,772). There are also many Filipinos (229,595) and immigrants from South America with Japanese ancestry (Joshua Project 2015; JCE6 2016, 123).

The Church in Japan

Japan has a low number of very small churches. Table 1 lists 9,039 churches in Japan [7,969 Protestant, 1,000 Catholic, and 70 Orthodox] (JCE6 2016, 11). Japan is far from a country saturated with churches, as there remain many unchurched areas. Twenty-four cities still do not have a single church. Over 1,800 rural areas including towns and villages linger without a church, of which nine hundred are considered strategic for establishing churches.

Also, ninety-six cities and forty-two towns and villages have only one church but are considered underchurched areas because the population exceeds twenty thousand people (CIS 2013, 5). Church Information Service has calculated there is one Protestant church for about sixteen thousand Japanese (CIS 2013, 4) making the average size of a church only thirty-four. Furthermore, most churches are indeed very small (see Table 2) with 82 percent of churches under fifty attendees, 62 percent under thirty attendees, and 31 percent under fifteen attendees (JMR 2015, 7).

Table 2. Size of Protestant Churches in Japan

Size of Churches (attendance)	Percentage of Total
Under 50 people	81.5%
Under 30 people	62.4%
Under 15 people	30.6%

Source: (JCE6 2016, 33)

These 9,039 churches are pastored by 11,703 professional clergy [10,198 Protestant, 1,451 Catholic, and 54 Orthodox] of which 1,009 are foreigners according to Table 3 (JCE6 2016,11).

Table 3. Japan Churches and Pastors

	Number of Churches	Pastors (foreign)
Catholic	1,000	1,451 (541)
Orthodox	70	54
Protestant	7,969	10,198 (468)
TOTAL	9,039	11,703 (1,009)

Source: (JCE6 2016, 11)

Seventy-two percent of these pastors are over sixty years old (see Figure 2). This and other factors contribute to a continued shortage of trained pastors to replace soon-to-be retired pastors and to fill current positions. Currently 3.8 percent of churches (300) still are without a pastor (*muboku*) and 7 percent of churches (560) share their pastor with another church (see Table 4). Some denominations are particularly hard hit with 20–40 percent without pastors (JCE6 2016, 45).

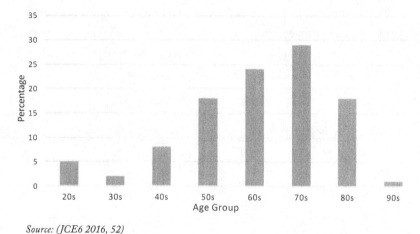

Source: (JCE6 2016, 52)

Figure 2. Pastoral Age

Table 4. Pastoral Shortage

	Pastors	Sharing Pastors (*kenmu*)	Without Pastors (*muboku*)
Number of Churches	6,670	560	300
Percentage	84.4%	7.1%	3.8%

Source: (JCE6 2016, 45)

The number of foreign missionaries serving in Japan is under 1,700 (JCE6 2016, 134). This is a decline from a peak of nearly 2,800 in the mid-1980s. In recent years, there has been an influx of missionaries from Asia especially South Korea. In a recent study 50 percent of missionaries reported their primary role to be church planting ministry (JMR 2015, 23–28).

Church Growth

The number of congregations in Japan increased for over seventy years, but recently this growth rate slowed to a near crawl. In a study of churches in Japan from 1945–1985, Toyotome calculated the average annual growth rate was 4.15 percent (1985, 230) but Montgomery determined the rate from 1960–1990 had dropped to 1.7 percent (1997, 18). Parrish assessed the average annual growth rate of Japanese churches from 1997–2007 as merely 0.10 percent (2008, 19). In the late 1980s, one new church was founded per forty to fifty churches; at the end of the 1990s, this ratio of existing churches to new churches had swelled to nearly 250.

For the last several years the net gain in churches has been a negative number in Japan. Exact causes for this decline are unknown, though churches have been closing at an alarming pace according to church researchers. In 2002, Mitsumori reported 271 churches closed, which is "the largest number in our experience" (2002, 6). No studies have been conducted, but the causes for church closings are assumed to be aging pastors and church members.

An earlier study of CIS church data of all Protestant denominations in Japan during the ten-year period from 1996 to 2007, 50 percent of the denominations were growing, 10 percent were remaining the same size, and 40 percent were declining (Mehn 2010, 9). These figures hold true whether the denomination is evangelical or charismatic while the conciliar The United Church of Christ in Japan (*Kyōdan*) had actually increased just slightly in total number of churches. Over this same period, the number of independent churches declined by 14 percent. A similar study with updated data from 1999–2014 (see Figure 3) shows overall decline continuing in the number of churches with over 65 percent of Japanese denominations leveling off or declining (JCE6 2016, 27–29).

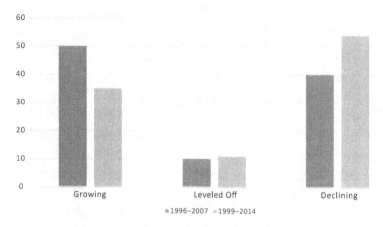

Source: (Mehn 2010, 9)

Figure 3. Decline of Denominations

After 150 years of Protestant mission, Japan remains relatively unreached by the gospel. Even the accelerated mission activity after World War II failed to substantially improve the situation (Hesselgrave 2005, 138). Kenneth Dale's 1996 evaluation of the spiritual soil of Japan as thorny is just as accurate today; in fact, the church in Japan may be in a worse overall situation. In the present climate, we cannot proceed with the status quo as it means the church in Japan would continue to decline. A few years ago, Parrish estimated that at the current rate, for Japan to reach a target of one church per one thousand people, an astronomical figure of nearly 2,800 years would be needed (2008, 19; see also Shibata 2016, 56–58).

Newer Vision

What is needed is not just the addition of fifty to sixty new churches each year but reproduction and even multiplication of the existing eight thousand churches and the planting of masses of new churches and movements. Braun shared this same outlook forty-five years ago, as "only a grand-scale church-planting enterprise" and the "multiplication of churches in large numbers is essential to the fulfilling of God's will for Japan" (Braun 1971, 27, 21).

Because of the vast need for more Japanese churches, key Japanese church leaders are calling for the growth of many more churches, not just the growth of bigger churches (Akae 1997, 106; Izuta 1998; Kishida 1992). Several feel the church "must plan on the winning of Japan by means of vastly multiplying the number of smaller churches" (Braun 1971, 28).

New types of smaller churches that are easy to birth and can reproduce early in their life cycle is needed. Changing the status quo will take radical commitment to risk-taking objectives, moving away from the exclusive clergy-led churches to many lay church plants, and a movement mentality. We must end the stalemate of just talking about church planting and the lack of obedient follow-through in the establishing of new churches.

To saturate Japan with churches at the rate of one church for 1,500 people, global missiologists have calculated from 50,000 to 120,000 churches would be necessary. Several visionary Japanese leaders have advanced a target number of churches corresponding to the number of convenience stores in Japan. Convenience stores now total over forty-three thousand, which is closing in on one store per two thousand population. Convenience store chains have studied population trends and done marketing research to maximize sales among a specific population in a carefully defined geographical area. Considering the number and location of these convenient stores could be helpful in developing strategic church planting plans and providing convenient churches for the masses of Japan.

REASONS FOR THE LACK OF RESPONSE IN JAPAN

Viewing the nation of Japan as a whole has stirred missiologist Ralph Winter to write, "There has never been a time when I have not considered Japan's hundreds of peoples mainly unreached people. Why? Because there is not yet a sufficiently Japanese church movement" (1997, 421). Many long for a day when the church in Japan will grow rapidly with movements of churches. At the same time, large hindrances to seeing movements of churches exist. Why does it seem the Japanese are unreceptive? Why is there a lack of church growth in Japan?

To answer these and similar questions dozens of possible approaches could be suggested. As the history of missions in Japan includes many deep discussions along these lines, no one simple answer has emerged. Many fine scholars have contributed various abstract and theoretical proposals, and that exploration needs to continue. For the purpose of this book we will look at three reasons that are not exclusive of each other but instead are overlapping.

1. The difficulty of contextualizing the gospel message for the Japanese culture.
2. The real challenges of spiritual resistance and warfare.
3. The health and relevance of the existing Christian church.

The first of these two will be discussed in this chapter. The third reason will be discussed in chapter two. Each chapter will lead quickly to practical applications for ministry.

THE DIFFICULTY OF CONTEXTUALIZING THE GOSPEL MESSAGE FOR THE JAPANESE CULTURE

Japanese worldview, belief system, and cultural elements have been extremely challenging in the history of Christian missions. The Japanese soil continues to present one of the greatest missiological challenges: how to bring the gospel to Japanese soil by seeding or transplanting it in such a way that it thrives. Though much seeding and transplanting of the gospel has occurred, the gospel has not taken sufficient root in Japanese soil.

Many Japanese still view Christianity as foreign and not an indigenous religion. Even a key Japanese leader has asserted, "My evaluation is that Japanese churches have largely failed to become Japanese in order to win the Japanese" (Fukuda 2015, 525). The incarnation of the gospel in Japanese soil should lead to a thriving indigenous church. Instead of being rooted in Japanese soil, many have concluded the church resembles a "potted plant" (Conn 1984, 246). Countless investigations on Christianity and the culture of Japan have been undertaken. The comprehensive discussion of contextualizing the gospel message for the Japanese culture is well beyond the scope of this book. We will give an overview of some key issues of the Japanese context to facilitate our reflection on several church case studies.

Religion in Japan

Most Japanese identify themselves as believers of both Shintoism and Buddhism. However, religion in Japan "is a variegated tapestry created by the interweaving of at least five major strands: Shinto, Buddhism, Daoism, Confucianism and folk religion" (Earhart 2014, 2). Shinto as a tribal faith is considered the backbone or religious bedrock upon which the rest of religion is based (Fujisawa 1958, 20–21). It is an animistic belief system meaning "the way of the *kami*" and is concerned with the gods or spirits, forces, and powers inhabiting a region and the nation of Japan.

Buddhism, originally from India, traveled through China and Korea before arriving in Japan in the sixth century. Although it was transplanted from outside, Buddhism underwent radical transformation in philosophy and practice to be considered Japanese. Mahayana Buddhism fully developed in Japan with five major schools of Tendai, Shingon, Jodo, Zen, and Nichiren, each having many subsects.

Daoism was never formally accepted as a religion in Japan, nevertheless its teachings on divination and life rhythms

influenced both Shintoism and Buddhism. Confucianism codi-
fied the basis for social order and filial piety.

While Shinto, Buddhism, Taoism, and Confucianism have
played their roles in Japanese religion, it is in folk religion that the
"various features of these religious and semi-religious systems were
blended to meet the spiritual needs of the common people, who
had to find religious meaning in the midst of their workaday life"
(Hori 1968: xi). Everyday Japanese are less interested in organized
religion but are very spiritual, finding fulfillment in the practical
outworking of folk religious practices (Macfarlane 2007, 175–177).

Religious Themes

Many encounter religious beliefs and practices in Japan that are
often complicated and sometimes ambiguous. These themes of religion in Japan reflect how beliefs influence practice in everyday life.

1. The closeness or immanence of the gods (*kami*),
   nature, and human beings rooted in traditional
   Shinto beliefs.
2. Ancestor worship. "Ordinary people accept ancestor
   worship as something beyond any particular religion
   or something encompassing all religions. . . . substantially it is their religion" (Chizuo 1985, 250).
   The belief and practices of ancestor worship have
   been described as the glue binding the Japanese
   to each other and to previous generations, hence
   supporting the Japanese household system (*ie*)
   throughout generations.
3. Importance of purification and avoiding pollution
   (Lewis 2013, 83–102).
4. Securing good fortune and avoiding misfortune
   through a host of folk religious practices including
   divination and amulets (Earhart 2014, 283–84).
5. Rites and local festivals marking significant seasons
   and rites of passage.

One comment should be made about the intimate connection between religion in Japan and the Japanese nation. As Buddhism and Shinto have long traditions and both were official religions of Japan at one time, Japanese national identity (*nihonkyō*) is interconnected with these religious systems. Former State Shintoism and its influence through the emperor system (*tennosei*) has contributed to a sense of national identity and religious character (Lee 1995, 118–123). "All of this added up to an ethnocentricity whereby the Japanese viewed themselves as the children of the gods, possessing a culture superior to any other" (Mathiesen 2006, 99). This is in part the source for a movement of cultural nationalism in pre-war Japan and a view of cultural uniqueness (*nihonjinron*) in post-war Japan (Sugimoto 2014, 16–24).

Religion in Japan is changing and, even as these themes remain very active, more Japanese continue to move away from organized religion. "The Japanese identification with gods in nature, the importance of the family, the significance of specific rituals and amulets, the prominence of individual cults—these all integrate religious activities into everyday life" (Earhart 2014, 15).

Contextualization

Considering the Japanese worldview and belief system, many feel the presentation of the gospel message needs significant adaption for the Japanese culture. Throughout the history of Christianity in Japan, many believers have made considerable sacrifices to relevantly bring the gospel of Jesus Christ to their countrymen. Their exemplary dedication in one of the most challenging missiological settings cannot be minimized. As a non-Japanese and non-expert in these areas, this writer feels uncomfortable to comment on these issues much beyond some reflections and observations.

The history of religious belief systems of Japan is largely a story of adaptions of foreign religions (Mullins 2006, 115). "As a relatively late-arrival, Christianity has perhaps had more difficulty in shedding its 'foreign' images and associations than has Buddhism and hence has remained a minority religion throughout its history in Japan" (Mullins 2006, 118). Robert Lee studied the Japanese church in the 1960s and concluded that for the Japanese the gospel is a "stranger in the land" of Japan and is viewed as very alien and foreign (Lee 1967, 163). Many like Winter believe this perspective is equally true today, contending "there is not yet a truly Japanese church movement but only a relatively small Westernized following" (Winter 2002, 8).

Because of Christianity's foreign stigma many have appealed for the need for critical contextualization in Japan (Fukuda 1993, 3). Regrettably, many Christian leaders in Japan lack a practical understanding of the concept and practice of contextualization. Moreau has defined contextualization as "the process whereby Christians adapt the forms, content and praxis of the Christian faith so as to communicate it to the minds and hearts of people with other cultural backgrounds. The goal is to make the Christian faith *as a whole*—not only the message but also the means of living out of our faith in the local setting—understandable" (Moreau 2005, 323).

Many find guidance to this contextualizing process in the ministry of the Apostle Paul, who in the first century ministered the gospel in a pluralistic cosmopolitan environment. A brief look at 1 Corinthians 9:16–23 can highlight the example of the Apostle Paul (Flemming 2005, 193–199). First, the priority and unchangeable nature of the gospel (vv. 16–17). The gospel message is to be proclaimed for the salvation of others. This becomes the personal burden, "Woe to me if I do not preach the gospel!" (v. 16). Our ultimate ministry goal is "for the sake of the gospel" (v. 23). Second, the task of personal adaption. Paul repeats five times "I became like" (vv. 20–22). The task is to incarnate and adapt our methods, and even ourselves, to connect the gospel with others. This demands a great personal sacrifice, such as "I made myself a slave" (v. 19). Third, we are to minister for effectiveness. Our desired outcome is "to win as many as possible" (v. 19). A simple summary of Pauline contextualization is the extent of work to contextualize. "I have become *all* things to *all* people so that by *all* possible means" [emphasis added] (v. 22). All this exertion and extent is that he "might save some" (v. 22), which is an unlimited investment for a limited outcome. The message to be proclaimed is the gospel. The method is ourselves, our *becoming* and our sacrifice. The reason is the pragmatic result of seeing others know Christ.

How can the church penetrate the Japanese culture causing the roots of the gospel to flourish in the soil of Japan? Critical contextualization exegetes both the scriptures and the context as "good contextualization draws on scripture as its primary source but recognizes the significant role that context will play in shaping theology and practice" (Ott & Strauss 2010, 283–84). It is an iterative process conducted in Christian community by examining the scriptures and investigating the context to determine how the gospel faithfully can be made understandable to every area of culture (Ott & Strauss 2010, 283–84).

Ultimate Commitment to Scripture

There is absolute truth, and we derive our authority from the scriptures. Contextualization involves viewing the context with theological lenses. In developing Christian answers for the Japanese worldview and culture[1] several theological areas will need review and possible emphasis, while other areas will need to be newly developed specifically for the Japanese context.

---

1. Contextualizing involves "theologizing" in the indigenous culture. Some theology rooted in Japanese experience has been developed by Kanzo Uchimura, Kazoh Kitamori, Toyohiko Kagawa, Kosuke Koyama, Shushaku Endo, and others—a complex topic too involved to cover adequately here. Readers are encouraged to study J. Nelson Jennings's article on "Japanese Theology" (2003) or, for a longer treatment, Yasuo Furuya's *A History of Japanese Theology* (1997).

1. A theology emphasizing the immanent nature of God while balancing his transcendence.
2. A theology of the sovereignty and love of God over and against fate and karma.
3. A theology of suffering and misfortune including a solid explanation of the problem of evil.
4. A theology of death and the departed beyond traditional Western personal eschatology.
5. A theology of the invisible world of powers, authorities, demons, and angels.
6. A theology of divine guidance over against divination.
7. A theology of man in his relationship to nature (the creation) and to the creator.
8. A theology of religious experience.

Respectful Commitment to Context

Though the context is secondary to Scripture, "we must be equally careful not to minimize the role of context" (Ott and Strauss 2010, 278). We are called to serve and love the Japanese people and so we must respect their feelings toward their values and beliefs. In critical contextualization, workers must choose what to do with cultural elements, whether the response should be adoption, rejection, modification, substitution, or toleration (Ott and Strauss 2010, 281–283).

Much hard work has already been done; however, several areas of Japanese culture need to be further understood, and subsequently contextualization needs to be applied, especially in rapid social change:

1. Gospel communication including everything from storytelling to effective preaching (Fukuda 2001, Hiebert 2012).
2. Determining and addressing felt needs (Dyer 2013, 127ff; Fukuda 1993, 183–87).

3. Japanese collectivism, social pressure, and the new individualism (Matsumoto 2002, 196–98).
4. Decision-making and conversion (Fukuda 1993).
5. Rituals and rites of passage, especially funerals (Fukuda 1993).

Japanese culture is often hard to determine, as the Japanese people fail to be very self-reflective of their culture and are reticent to speak to people they do not know well regarding their cultural views. Also, globalization is a reality for Japanese and makes our contextualization more of a challenge (Ott 2015). So much more street-level investigation is necessary. Possibly, Christian "returnees" returning from living in other countries could be helpful in providing reflection on the Japanese culture.

The Danger of Syncretism

In the process of indigenizing or inculturating the gospel into a culture, it is possible the gospel may be compromised. As we learned from Paul in 1 Corinthians 9, the gospel must remain the priority in adaption as God's absolute truth or it may lose its prophetic power. "Syncretism occurs when the purity of the Gospel message or the essential functions of the church are sacrificed at the altar of relevance" (Ott & Wilson 2011, 124). The Japanese are noted to quickly adopt religious ideas and include them in their belief systems. As Christianity is a religion of exclusive belief in Jesus Christ, the gospel can be an offense to unbelievers. So many are tempted to compromise with the culture and enter the road into syncretism, which can lead to false doctrine and heresy. For example, some scholars see that the *Kakure Kirishitan* (hidden Christians), who practiced Christianity in secret due to persecution during the Edo Period (1603-1868), intermingled Christian truth and practice with Buddhism, Japanese folk religion, and Mariolatry (Jennings 2003, 184; Miyazaki 2003, 22, 31; Furuya 2006, 42–45).

Making Religion Practical

Many Japanese see Christianity as appealing to an intellectual elite and have accused Christianity of being *ronripoi* or "too logical." For Japanese the only "logic" of their religion is that it effectively meets their needs. In their book, *Practically Religious: Worldly Benefits and the Common Religion of Japan,* Reader and Tanabe argue the central element to Japanese religion is *genze riyaku,* which means "this-worldly benefits" or "practical benefits in this lifetime." The practical benefits of religion are "primarily material or physical gains such as good health, healing, success, or . . . personal advancement in one's life path, . . . personal well-being and freedom from problems" (Reader & Tanabe 1998, 2). In contextualizing the gospel for Japan, we dare not abdicate the rigorous intellectual basis of our beliefs based on the truth of Scripture. But at the same time, we must denounce dead orthodoxy, lament an absence of "heart religion," and resist the promotion of a prosperity gospel. Practical experiential religion emanating from a lifestyle of Christian discipleship, obedience of the truth, and missional engagement must be persistently demonstrated in the Japanese context.

Summary

Japan presents many challenges to contextualizing the gospel. Japanese adhere to many religious themes, yet their understanding of their religion is often unstructured, defies analysis, adapts by making use of many elements, and is intensely practical. To communicate the gospel to the minds and hearts of Japanese demands holistic and rigorous commitment by Christians. "By rooting all theology and practice in scripture, penetrating to the level of worldview, and interacting with every aspect of context, we can help ensure the emergence of healthy churches that connect with and transform their worlds" (Ott & Strauss 2010, 290).

THE REAL CHALLENGES OF SPIRITUAL RESISTANCE AND WARFARE

The second reason the Japanese have failed to respond to the gospel and why a vibrant church movement has not occurred in Japan is due to spiritual resistance and warfare. The main hindrance to the response and growth in Japan is not just conceptual, cultural, or practical but ultimately spiritual. Evangelism is dependent on the Holy Spirit's conviction of sin, righteousness, and judgment (John 16:8). Discipling and the planting of the church are fundamentally spiritual tasks. "Mission is ultimately a spiritual task that must be empowered with spiritual resources" (Ott & Strauss 2010, 246). We must remember all ministry is wholly dependent on God's sovereign "work."

The Christian's struggle is against the three spiritual enemies of the flesh, the world, and the devil and evil spiritual forces. Our ministry in reaching Japan is "to open their eyes and turn them from darkness to light, and from the power of Satan to God that they may receive forgiveness of sins" (Acts 26:18). Paul sees this as a spiritual conflict needing dependence on God and his resources. "Finally, be strong in the Lord and in his mighty power. Put on the full armor of God, so that you can take your stand against the devil's schemes. For our struggle is not against flesh and blood, but against the rulers, against the authorities, against the powers of this dark world and against the spiritual forces of evil in the heavenly realms" (Eph 6:10–12). There is a spiritual battle to stand against the devil and other opposing forces of evil.

Biblical Worldview

To focus on this conflict appropriately, all believers must have a clear biblical worldview. Modernism and naturalism deny the supernatural including God himself, personal spiritual beings like angels, and miracles. For the Christian this supernatural world does indeed exist. God dwells in heaven, and man created with a spiritual nature lives on the miraculously created earth. For many in the West this is the practical extent of what they consider the spiritual dimension. What is neglected is the dimension inhabited by obedient angels and rebellious Satan and demons, what Hiebert has called the "excluded middle." Westerners often exclude the middle level of supernatural this-worldly beings and forces from their worldview (Hiebert 1982, 43). The spiritual world begins with the almighty God, the creator of the cosmos, who is omnipotent and complete in love. Part of the creation is God's loyal kingdom servants and personal spiritual agents: the angels. Also a fallen part of God's creation are the rebellious spiritual entities opposed to God's Kingdom: the devil and demons. The battleground of this spiritual conflict is over the souls of people and their related human systems and structures.

Resistance

There is evil in our world that comes from fallen man and the work of Satan and demons. Man is fallen due to sin, by nature and by choice, and is resistant to the creator God. This fallenness affects everything including truth perception, knowing God, the focus of worship, and social relationships. Paul in Romans chapter one reveals this downward spiral (v. 18) and its effect on man and his perceptions (v. 21). Man's wickedness causes the truth to be suppressed, hearts to become darkened, and minds to be given up to depravity (v. 28). Paul asserts that God has clearly revealed himself as a powerful creator but fallen man has exchanged God's glory for images and they worshiped "created things rather than the creator" (vv. 19,20,25). The sin of man is both individual and corporate. Human rebellion against God manifests itself in human systems that do not glorify God. The widespread idol worship throughout Japan is ample evidence of Paul's teaching in contemporary times.

Resistance also comes from Satan, a fallen angel. Satan is a personal spiritual being plotting evil with other fallen angels, the demons. These spiritual opponents are real. Satan is actively blinding the eyes of unbelievers (2 Cor 4:4), snatching God's word from their hearts (Luke 8:12), and generally hindering the gospel and oppressing people as the prince of this world (John 12:31; 14:30; 16:11; 1 John 5:19). Demons enslave man through "the basic principles of the world" (Gal 4:3; Col 2:8, 20) and influence and possess certain individuals. Countless examples from Japan would attest to Satan and his demons and their stratagems of repressing Japan in spiritual darkness.

For the last twenty-five years much healthy debate and disagreement has occurred regarding various aspects of the spiritual warfare movement, especially the deliverance model of spiritual warfare and exorcism (Beilby & Eddy 2012, 2, 36). Concern for several errors and excesses led the Lausanne Movement to issue a *Statement on Spiritual Warfare* (Lausanne 1993). The Strategic Level Spiritual Warfare movement espoused by Peter Wagner and others promotes spiritually mapping a local area with the intent of "binding" the residing territorial spirits. Several scholars have concerns about these teachings on territorial spirits and strongholds as they may be introducing animistic or tribal beliefs into the Christian worldview (Ott & Strauss 2010, 260–261). These excesses have been a potential problem in Japan. While these and other aspects of spiritual warfare demand our caution and discernment the spiritual realm should not be completely ignored (1 John 4:1–3).

Implications of Spiritual Warfare

1. The Sovereign Lord of Scripture is ultimately in control of the cosmos, not Satan or any other spiritual being. Christ will eventually unify all things in creation (Eph 1:9–10).

2. God is infinitely more powerful than created Satan (Eph 1:19–20). There is not a cosmic dualism.

3. As King, Jesus has been given "All authority in heaven and on earth" (Matt 28:18) and has triumphed over all in the Cross

"having disarmed the powers and authorities, he made a public spectacle of them, triumphing over them by the Cross" (Col 2:15; cf. Eph 1:21–23). The purpose of the Cross was that "by his death he might break the power of him who holds the power of death— that is, the devil" (Heb 2:14). The name of Jesus has authority over Satan and his demons. Jesus appeared to "destroy the devil's work" (1 John 3:8).

4.   Believers are not to fear spiritual entities. John encouraged, "You, dear children, are from God and have overcome them, because the one who is in you is greater than the one who is in the world" (1 John 4:4). Believers do not fight for victory, but from an already achieved victory.

5.   Christians do not fight alone, but together. Ephesians 6 was written to an entire church in an entire city. We stand and fight together. Christ's victory involves his church (Eph 1:22–23, 3:10–11).

Japan's Spiritual Environment

Anyone concerned with reaching the Japanese with the gospel will soon become familiar with the reality of spiritual darkness in Japan. With idolatry visible just about everywhere and religious practices pervasive, Japan is clearly a country of spiritual darkness. Born with original sin, individuals continue in their fallen state by rebelling against God. This depravity manifests itself throughout whole societies (Rom 1:18–32). Satan, the father of lies, the spiritual father of all unbelievers (John 8:44), and the "god of this age," "has blinded the minds of unbelievers, so that they cannot see the light of the Gospel that displays the glory of Christ, who is the image of God" (2 Cor 4:4).

Many Japanese live in the "excluded middle" of unseen spirits and forces. Japanese believe in a large pantheon of spiritual beings such as lonely spirits (*muenbotoke*), ghosts (*obake*), wandering spirits (*yurei*), dead ancestors (*hotoke*), and powers within inanimate objects and impersonal forces such as fate, all of which control their lives. Their practical religion of animism and spiritism exposes them to more delusion by Satan and demons. Their enslavement to idolatry is more like that observed by the Old Testament prophets.

Those who have ministered in Japan have probably seen or experienced the reality of this spiritual darkness and enslavement. This is often sensed when families welcome back the spirits of their ancestors during the summer period of *obon*, around temples and shrines especially when people are observing religious practices, and nearby places of occult activity such as palm reading or divination. But at the same time, it would be hard to describe just what is going on in the spirit world as it is unclear from the scriptures and from experience. In spiritual warfare, we must always remember "our massive ignorance" and the "fog of war" (Beilby & Eddy 2012, 117).

The Armor of God

Paul reminds us of this spiritual warfare in Ephesians 6:13–17 and includes a list of God's armor of truth, gospel, righteousness, faith, and salvation, all for defense, that are given to the believer due to the work of Christ. This armor prepares the believer to stand, which is repeated four times in Ephesians chapter six. In spiritual conflict believers need to be aware of the authority and presence of Christ (Matt 28:18, 20), that he "rescued us from the dominion of darkness" (Col 1:13) and due to the Cross our Lord has triumphed over all spiritual enemies (Col 2:15).

Besides the armor for defense, the believer is also given the word of God as a weapon for offense (Eph 6:17). Using the word of God, we conduct a "truth encounter" with unbelievers.

> For though we live in the world, we do not wage war as the world does. The weapons we fight with are not the weapons of the world. On the contrary, they have divine power to demolish

strongholds. We demolish arguments and every
pretension that sets itself up against the knowledge of God, and we take captive every thought
to make it obedient to Christ. (2 Cor 10:3–5)

Our task is preaching the truth of the gospel to ourselves and
others.

The Weapon of Prayer

Spiritual warfare in Ephesians 6 is in the context of intercessory
prayer for believers to advance the gospel (Eph 6:18–20). Paul
requests prayer for boldness and fearlessness for him in proclaiming
the gospel. Prayer is an essential element in the advance of the
gospel and the church. "Prayer is designed to extend the kingdom
into fruitless enemy territory" (Piper 2010, 69). Rather than
praying against spirits, the kind of biblical prayers needed are that
God would open the eyes of people in darkness and lead them in
repentance for their rebellion against him.

Praying for a Breakthrough

Christian believers need to pray for the nations to come to God:
"Ask me, and I will make the nations your inheritance, the ends
of the earth your possession" (Ps 2:8). Historical breakthroughs
have happened in other countries resulting in many conversions
and an explosion of churches. These missiological breakthroughs
and church planting movements are an act of God. David Bryant
writes, the "evangelical scholar J. Edwin Orr summarized into
one simple statement his sixty years of historical study on great
prayer movements preceding spiritual awakenings: 'When God is
ready to do something new with his people, he always sets them
to praying'" (Bryant 1995, 30–31).

Our essential role is beseeching God and interceding for
the Japanese people. An emphasis on prayer for God's blessing
and breakthrough in the Arab Muslim world and the former
Soviet Union went on for many years and the missiological

breakthroughs came. Many are hoping God will bring a spiritual breakthrough to Japan like God has done for other people groups in Asia. Mongolia went from four Christians in 1989 to over fifty thousand today, and Korea's Christian population grew from 2 percent to 29 percent in less than fifty years. Garrison has found that prayer for workers, church leaders, and gospel advance are essential (Garrison 2004, 172, 173, 175–177). Believers around the world need to harness a new movement of prayer on behalf of the Japanese people for the glory of God!

The role of prayer emanates from a confidence about the outcome of the battle between God and Satan. Intercession should be "big prayers" that the gospel would advance, the rule and reign of God through his kingdom would come, and Christ will build his church (Matt 16:18). "No church-planting movement will rise above the prayer ministry of those involved with it" (Ott and Wilson 2009, 181). Praying for Japan could include prayer for the following:

- God would send workers into the harvest field of Japan (Matt 9:38). There is a shortage of pastors and the number of missionaries has declined.
- God would open spiritual eyes by removing the deceit of the enemy (2 Cor 4:4).
- People would turn to the true God and repent of idolatry.
- Japanese would no longer worship the spirits of their ancestors.
- God would grant believers boldness (Eph 6:19) amid social pressure to conform.
- Japanese would seek guidance from the biblical God (Jer 33:3) and not from divination and fortune-telling.
- Religious freedom from government restrictions would continue.

- Traditional religious values of Japan including Shintoism and the Emperor System would be questioned and rejected.
- God would bring multiple church planting movements to Japan.
- God would renew and revive all Christians and churches.

Summary

The Japanese church has been courageous and believers have been persistent amongst a country permeated with spiritual darkness. In a country with only a few communities of Christian faith to share the truth of the Word of God, Japan is spiritually starving. The task of multiplying the church is a spiritual struggle against spiritual resistance. In understanding spiritual warfare we must be thoroughly biblical, avoid basing our beliefs on subjective personal experience, and shun sensationalistic practices. Christian believers are called to dependence on the Holy Spirit, alertness in battle, and prayerfulness, knowing the ultimate and final victory was won by Christ on the Cross.

In this chapter, we have considered two external reasons for the lack of responsiveness to the gospel: inadequate contextualization of the gospel in Japanese culture and spiritual resistance and warfare. Kenneth Dale has accurately described the source of the problem as both (1) the Japanese culture and (2) the existing church, which lacks engagement and contextualization with the culture (1996). The next chapter will consider the internal reason for the lack of rapid church growth: the health and relevance of the existing Christian church.

THE CHURCH IN
JAPANESE SOIL

The last chapter introduced three reasons for the lack of response to missions in Japan. We began by looking at gospel penetration in Japanese soil. We considered two external factors: (1) the issue of acculturation and contextualization into Japanese culture and (2) spiritual resistance and warfare. This chapter will consider the third reason for lack of growth and health of churches in Japanese soil: the health and relevance of the Christian church.

This lack of growth of the gospel in Japan is attributed not just to the external context of Japanese culture and spiritual resistance, but also to the internal context of the Japanese church itself. Some even feel that "the growth of the Church is often affected as much by internal factors operating within the Churches themselves as by prevailing social and political conditions" (Braun 1971, 170). As a result of historical studies and field research on the church in Japan, several have pointed out that overall the Japanese church is not healthy, and this lack of health prevents church growth. "The slow growth of the Church in Japan is due not only to the disinclination of the Japanese to become Christian, but to the cumbersome and faulty way in which the Church goes about its task" (Braun 1971, 19). Over decades, many writers like Braun have cited the church as a key reason for the lack of responsiveness and church growth in Japan (see Lee 1967; Conrad 1988; Dale 1996; Sherrill 2002). And more recently some Japanese leaders are very disapproving of their Japanese church asserting that "The church in Japan does not embody the heart of Christ for the church" (Research F Group 2012, 11–15).

What follows is a summary of several key issues and factors within the existing church in Japan. This is not an exhaustive summary, but these are some reasons for the lack of evangelism, discipling, growth, and reproduction of churches. The underlying reasons, namely the lack of faithful application of essential biblical principles, are paralleled in churches of other countries and among other people groups. But each of these reasons for the lack of healthy growing churches may be reinforced by Japanese culture and even some Japanese church practices. The following factors should be viewed as being interrelated barriers to the health and growth of the church. They are stated as imperatives for needed change in the Japanese church.

Before we begin this section, a word of caution is in order. The purpose of this section is not to overly criticize and take wild potshots at the existing church in Japan. We respect the many leaders and members who have been faithful to God in developing the church in Japan. At the same time, many in leadership hold a "holy dissatisfaction" with the Japanese church in its current state. While respecting the church historically as the Bride of Christ, many also feel compelled to meticulously examine the existing church through biblical and missiological lenses.

As the subject of this book is new churches, the link between new churches and the existing church will be continually discussed in the chapters that follow, especially chapters on effective models to reproduce churches (chapter five) and leadership for reproduction (chapter six). The following are six interrelated directions for the existing church as it moves into the future.

1. Shift Church Leadership
2. Develop the Church as the People of God
3. Engage Local Communities
4. Produce Holistic Disciples
5. Partner with Others in Unity
6. Recover the Church's Mission

SHIFT CHURCH LEADERSHIP

First, Japanese churches need to shift from a clergy-centric leadership to a more broad-based leadership that mobilizes all members of the church.

Clergy-centric leadership is a problem among many churches globally. Many writers have cited this as one of the biggest problems in Japanese churches, affecting evangelism, growth of disciples and leaders, and reproduction of the church (Braun 1971, 107–110; Dale 1975, 158–59; OC International Japan 1993, 14; Sherrill 2002). A broad clergy-lay gap prevents ministry growth beyond one person, thus keeping churches small (average 35) and not reproducing.

Japanese leadership is heavily influenced by Confucian ethics and social order—based on the five relationships—and by Samurai (*Bushidō*) value (Lee 1999, 75). The resultant Japanese social structure reinforces leadership characterized by top-down hierarchy, formal leadership, authority based on position, and leader-follower relationships grounded on obligation (see Figure 11 on page 139). Between the leader and follower, "strong emotions tie the hierarchy together through a cultural system of loyalty (*chugi*) from the bottom and paternalistic obligation (*onjo-shugi*) from the top" (Matsumoto 2002, 12).

Church leadership itself has been categorized with a large clergy-laity gap due to Confucian relationships of teacher over disciple and senior over junior. Several decades ago many observed that the typical church was a mini-fiefdom with the pastor acting as a feudal lord. Ohashi believes that the clergy-laity "gap" remains a systemic problem in the training of current church leaders, and the traditional structure of the church causes some people to be viewed as elite and others more common (Ohashi 2007, 142–43). Some would identify this with a Roman Catholic view of church leadership where the church does not exist without the presence of the bishop or priest.

Japanese pastors often emphasize positional leadership of the pastoral office that manifests itself through what Lewis calls the "Sensei syndrome" (Lewis 2013, 261–65). Pastor-leaders are viewed as elite with their formal academic training and their full-time employment as a religious professional. Through the emphasis on positional leadership, the laity are not frequently empowered for ministry, which results in followers that are passive and often lack desire to be a "leader." Other evidences are little ministry delegation and members that are not mobilized for ministry. Believers are encouraged to merely help the pastor with his ministry. Church ministry is often conducted by *sola pastora* (a sole pastor) who drives, as the Japanese call it, the "one-man bus." This could explain why the majority of churches in Japan are considered single-celled, with an average attendance of thirty-five, while the most common size of churches is closer to eighteen people.

To shift church leadership in the Japanese church several have suggested possible answers.

- Many have called for a new theological shift regarding church leadership in Japan where a culture of hierarchical relationships is unlikely to change. They recognize that church leadership still must be exercised by an ever-growing number of individuals but that the elitist approach to leadership be eliminated. Even churches that consider themselves "high church" promote various leadership positions in the church besides the senior pastor. They hold that biblical pastoral leadership does not require formal seminary training, working full-time, or having ministry credentials. Japan is a culture with a high power distance (PD) or distance between leader and follower (Hofstede 1997, 28). Many effective leaders in Japan see a church leader as *primus inter pares* (first among equals) and lower the high leadership pyramid (see

Figures 11 and 12 on page 139), thereby lowering the PD factor. Some pastors refuse to be called "senior pastor," and others insist that lay people serving as church staff also be called pastor. In one case, a Japanese pastor of a cell church put himself under one of his cell leaders for accountability.

- Others have called for a shift to a more broad-based system of leadership with many new kinds of leaders. Braun and others have suggested multiple levels of leadership in local churches based on experience and gifting. Many see more opportunities for lay people to become interns, staff members, ministry team leaders, and small group leaders. More leadership development could result in more church reproduction. Jiro Chida has wisely affirmed, "church planting is leadership development."

- Many have called for a shift in the pastoral leadership role to focus more on empowerment of the laity for ministry. For clergy "to equip the saints for the work of the ministry" (Eph 4:11 NET) would mean not an elimination of the clergy but a shift in the role of the clergy to equip the laity by entrusting and empowering them with ministry (see Otomo 2016, 26–27).

National Church Development (NCD) has conducted wide research on hundreds of churches in Japan. Among the eight factors in healthy churches, they have determined that "empowering leadership" was the weakest factor for the church in Japan. Field research in Japan on reproducing churches has shown that there are healthy churches developing both lay and clergy leaders and sending them out in ministry. Their leadership is characterized by empowerment and developing leadership for ministry (Mehn 2013, 186). This is the "priesthood of all believers" not in theory but in actual practice of mobilization of church members.

> The role of the clergy, then, is not so much to
> do the work of the Church, as to equip believers
> so *they* can do this work. If this could be fully
> understood in Japan . . . and put into practice,
> the life of the Church would be revolutionized.
> One recognizes that this will not be easy, for the
> training of the clergy in the seminaries is not at
> all designed to prepare them for this kind of role
> (Braun 1971, 109).

Though some of the above suggested changes and shifts may seem radical to some, there are many churches in Japan that have implemented several of these directions and consequently found new reasons for growth. We will return to the subject of leadership for church reproduction in chapter six.

DEVELOP THE CHURCH AS THE PEOPLE OF GOD

Second, Japanese churches need to develop the church less as a religious institution and more as the people of God.

As a church grows and ages, its nature as a dynamic living organism with simple structures can gradually be lost by movement towards static organization and even institutionalization. Japanese culture has a comfortable tendency to view the world in terms of organization, bureaucracy, form, or structure. One cultural example is Japanese archery. Its primary task is not necessarily to hit the bullseye but to ensure proper form, culminating in the arrow's release.

This Japanese tendency to emphasize structural nature, in contrast to organic and relational nature, is no less true for the church. The biblical concept of the church as a gathered community can be lost in a schedule of meetings and events in church buildings. The Japanese church needs to powerfully demonstrate itself as a relational group with a spiritual consciousness

(Dyer 2013, 116–117), more like a warm family than a static organization.

Ask Japanese believers what a church is, and the default answer is often defined in terms of scheduled events, building locations, and organization. This contrasts with the church defined as individuals living out a special relationship as God's people with unique qualities and positions (1 Pet 2:9,10). Otherwise, the phrase "let's be the church" then becomes replaced by "let's go to church." The organic church as the family of God is replaced with an organization; the people of God with a building; the body of Christ with a list of activities.

The highly relational aspect of Japanese culture can be captured to develop the church (Dyer 2013, 70). The church can be experienced more as a way of life together (Acts 2:42–47) rather than organization and meetings. Japan has several healthy churches exemplifying strong relational ties and deep caring for each other. This relational focus is essential as evangelism, discipleship, and leadership development are all relational processes.

Some have suggested possible means to focus on the people of God.

- Leadership should emphasize this relational nature of the church more than the organizational nature. The leaders of churches that are reproducing in Japan have a strong view of the church not merely as a static organization but as a dynamic living organism (Mehn 2010, 109–10).
- The focus on the church as the people of God increases as small groups (or cell groups) emphasize spiritual care in warm relationships (Lewis 2013, 247–51). Many churches with small groups are healthy and growing in Japan, which is a highly relational and collectivistic culture. These groups increase pastoral care, stimulate more outreach, and provide avenues for more leaders to be mobilized.

- The church as the people of God is especially helpful in engaging people in the community. Strong relationships touch people in the community with evangelism in word and deed. In increasingly urbanized Japan, current personal and social issues such as suicide, *hikikomori* (acute social withdrawal syndrome), sexless marriages, bullying, harassment, and emotional and psychological problems indicate the urgent need for deep caring relationships within a community (McQuilken 2007, 63–64). The church is poised to meet some of these needs and provide personal support to those struggling with these issues.

ENGAGE LOCAL COMMUNITIES

Third, churches in Japan need to become more relevant and engaged in their local community settings.

Kenneth Dale has accurately described the reasons for the paucity of growth of the gospel in Japan as both (1) the Japanese culture and (2) the existing church, which lacks engagement and contextualization with the culture (Dale 1996, 1). The core issues are unavoidable at the local level. Many outside local churches feel the church is not connected to them as "its matters are of no interest and appear merely as ingrown self-interest" (Dale 1998, 285).

Many reasons could be stated for this lack of engagement, such as the size of the church, insufficient energy or resources, and maybe an inferiority complex. The fortress mentality of the church and the risks of compromise with the culture have also been suggested. Also, in some historical periods, the culture and even the government of Japan have been antithetical to the growth of Christian churches.

The problem of churches and their lack of relational connection with their communities is illustrated by Jacobsen, who many years ago found that 87.3 percent of all churches had never conducted a survey of their community (Jacobsen 1977, 5). That has not changed much over the years, as shown from recent surveys of Japanese communities. The Elijah Group conducted field research that indicated many Japanese are completely unaware of Christian churches even if a church meets in their own community (Elijah Kai 2009, 445). According to research by Christian Relief, Assistance, Support, and Hope (CRASH), about 60 percent of the churches in Tokyo are not connected with their communities or surrounding churches.

One reason that the church appears culturally irrelevant is that it continues with outdated patterns and forms that were possibly relevant in previous decades. Public worship services, often the first place where non-Christians attend, are not sensitive to newcomers or seekers. Churches need to be constantly developing rather than remaining static museums. "There is little that is creative, adapted to culture and local needs, little that is attractive to outsiders. There is need to make our worship and meetings more joyful, open, and flexible" (Dale 1996, 14).

The end result is that the majority of Japanese churches are outdated and irrelevant in their own communities. Jesus calls his people to be the salt of the earth and the light of the world (Matt 5: 13–16). Instead of becoming a transplanted tree, the church appears more like a stunted *bonsai* plant in a pot.

However, there are encouraging signs pointing churches to engage their communities and become relevant.

- Many church leaders have evaluated the strengths and weaknesses of the attractional evangelism model for churches in Japan. Along with developing programs to get people to come to church events, churches are developing programs where "the church" is brought to the community. Many churches use community centers, coffee shops, and other neutral locations for outreach to children, youth, mothers, businessmen, and adults through seminars, clubs, the arts, English classes, and the like.

- Various churches are connecting with their communities through relevant outreach for community needs. Several of these are after school programs, daycare for the aged, help for people with emotional troubles, counseling for couples and parents, and help for *hikikomori* youth and parents. Many more needs like these should be explored and discovered by the whole Japanese church.
- Recent national disasters have awakened churches to engage in ministry in their communities. Destruction caused by the Great Hanshin Earthquake in Kobe (1995) forced many to a transformed understanding of the church—its connection with the community and determination to be better mobilized for disaster on a national level. After the 2011 Great Northeast triple disaster, many churches from outside the disaster area sent volunteer teams to conduct relief work among disaster victims. These church members returned from the disaster area sensitized to the needs of people outside their own church and desired to similarly engage people in their local communities. Disaster relief ministry will be discussed further in chapter four.
- Though introduced to Japan very recently, the early adoption of a "missional community" model for churches is encouraging. Developing the church family around their local community with the expressed purpose to engage it has great promise to keep the church relevant.

Each local church in its setting has limited energy toward cultural engagement and contextualization. The key is to preserve the truth while finding new wineskins for the church (Luke 5:37–38). The reformed church is constantly reforming to lovingly engage their communities and be outwardly oriented to them in mission. May each church find at least one relevant community need where it can penetrate the culture and transform it.

PRODUCE HOLISTIC DISCIPLES

Fourth, Japanese believers need to be developed as joyful passionate incarnations of the good news.

The gospel is not only the good news of God's salvation for those who have not yet believed in Christ; it is also the message of promise for believers to be empowered for ongoing growth and transformation. That personal renewal is the source for transforming the communities where we live. Walking in this gospel in the culture of Japan presents many unique challenges for individual believers.

The collectivistic culture of Japan demands individual conformity to expectations of the group. Because Japan is also a hierarchical culture, individuals are obligated to externally perform for the group, particularly for their leaders and seniors. This sense of social obligation is a constant dynamic in all interpersonal relationships in Japan and is a dimension of religion. This leads some Christian believers into exhaustion from external performance-driven diligence, especially among churches where legalism and perfectionism are encouraged and taught. This self-generated perseverance without the application of the gospel of biblical grace leaves believers with the path of "just trying harder" to look good before God and other believers.

In relating to the requirements and laws of God, disciples are to avoid both errors of antinomianism and legalism. The grace of the gospel includes both salvation from the penalty of sin and freedom from the power of sin so believers can walk in deeper sanctification and obedience. Christians experience this freedom that grows out of a deeper understanding of God's amazing love and grace, leading to motivation to follow God, which in turn grows. Rather than mere external obedience to scriptural commands in order to earn God's favor, grace produces obedience at deeper heart levels that empowers more outward changes. This inner heart motivation connects their faith to dependence on God's indwelling Holy Spirit and his guidance, renewing, equipping, filling, instructing, and empowering.

The burden to conform and to be accepted also weighs heavily on Japanese leaders, who normally shun ministry risk for safety reasons, while others settle for second best or even teeter on resignation of ministry. For Christian leaders and workers, the seeming lack of "ministry success" drains life's energy by developing a pattern where they believe God is only pleased with their dedication and efforts instead of resting on the truths of the gospel where we are righteous and accepted in God's sight on the basis of the work of Christ for us.

As a minority in Japanese culture, many Christian believers struggle with being socially accepted by others, which often overrides their unique spiritual identity as being loved by God as his adopted children. This can likewise eclipse their sense of personal value before God in the gift of righteousness through justification by faith. Moreover, this struggle can even extinguish any Christian joy in their hearts brought to them from the lavish promises of the gospel of Christ.

These underlying spiritual formation or inner soul issues manifest themselves in many personal relationships among Japanese Christians. For some it is an unforgiving spirit which will affect their marriage, their relationships with parents, children, and extended family, or their church life. For others, it is a relentless drive for the approval of other people instead of the approval of God brought to them through their union with his Son.

Many of the world's collectivistic cultures are very supportive of the individual. But the dark side of collectivism is often evident in Japan with the pressure from one's group resulting in death from overwork (*karōshi*), domestic violence, alcoholism, and many with emotional breakdowns, anxiety disorders, depression, and even suicide.

There is a very high threshold for a Japanese to become a member of a church. Later, when these new believers feel they have failed and so lose face, the path from shame to save them honor is to simply quit or "leave the church by the backdoor." Other Japanese finally give in to the unrelenting social pressure and leave the faith. Researchers report that "probably 1–2% of the Japanese population has "graduated from Christianity." McQuilken believes that "80 percent of those baptized disappear within a decade" (McQuilken 2007, 50). These are people who at one time attended church, enrolled as a "seeker" in a church, and may even have been baptized as a believer, but then over time left Christianity. Matsunaga, retired head of the largest Protestant seminary in Japan, revealed research stating that few people continue as active Christians past 2.8 years after their baptism. He insists that more effort is necessary to provide pastoral care, nurturing, and training in the Christian life (Matsunaga 1999, 299). In sum, though the threshold is seemingly high to get into the church, it is relatively easy to go out the backdoor, which is a situation that in an ideal world should be the reverse.

Within the Japanese culture there are several solutions proposed to help form stronger and more holistic disciples.

Demonstrate discipleship as a lifestyle, not just Christian knowledge

In the early introduction of the church in Japan, missionaries used a "school approach" to plant the church. Many students and educated people were reached through an approach that used lectures, discussions, and study (Yamamori 1974, 57–58). This church-as-school approach, often linked with Christian schools, continues to profoundly influence the church in Japan to this day (Miyamoto 2008, 160). Many believers and non-Christians see discipleship and the church (*kyōkai* [teaching association or study society]) as simply mastering a body of information.

Discipleship should be more than an invitation to be more religious by simply adding knowledge but a personal journey of following the risen Christ. Discipleship should be fellowshipping with God, walking in his Spirit, and a lifestyle of applying what is learned in the journey. Jesus taught his disciples to teach other disciples "to obey everything I have taught you" (Matt 28:20). Disciples were to live out each day of the Christian life comprehensively as it relates to work, community, or school. Discipleship is engaged with all of life. Regrettably, many have commented that Christianity in Japan is too logical and not practical, while Jesus expected a more experiential and practical religion. This could be one possible reason why some churches and movements seem to be growing faster in Japan as they may place more emphasis on experiential religion.

Cultivate theological foundations for the inner spiritual life

For many the path of following Jesus in Japan is characterized more by external behavior nurtured by legalism, moralism, and, in the extreme sense, separatism rather than belief in the good news of grace. Often church life in Japan is lightheartedly described as the 3 K's of *kurai* (dark), *katai* (stiff), and *kibishii* (strict). Many believers and churches need to again cultivate an inner spiritual life of the heart "to grow in the grace and the knowledge of our Lord and savior Jesus Christ" (2 Pet 3:18).

On earth, Jesus succeeded in perfectly obeying God and living a godly life of service. On the Cross, Jesus completely removed our shame and uncleanliness. We have no fear of shame or rejection, as his perfect rightness is ours by faith. The believer's faith in Christ's death on the Cross and his resurrection will bring freedom and joy in Christ through continual repentance and dependence on the Holy Spirit. These truths overcome personal failure and spur growth in brokenness and humility leading to thankfulness and transformation. This merciful gospel is the believer's source for forgiving others, resolving conflict, and loving others through peacemaking.

Instead of slavishly following Japanese cultural beliefs that negatively affect their inner spiritual life but rather applying the transforming power of the gospel (Rom 1:16), Christians would learn to replace cold performance with warm-hearted obedience, learn to persevere not by grit but solely "in faith," and replace heartless obligation with the fullness of grace. By integrating these theological truths as spiritual formation, they would cultivate their inner life motivations, and then their true joy and hope would be found in Christ alone and not from outward conformity to their group.

Every believer experiences brokenness and failure and requires forgiveness from both God and man. So, every believer must continually depend on God's mercy. Growing as disciples is not merely information or external behavior but inner transformation through the conviction and sanctification of the Spirit. This transformation from the inside out should be modeled by leaders and lived out by all believers in gospel community.

Develop disciples through coaching and mentoring

For many Japanese churches processes of discipleship are limited, and few churches in Japan have more than a baptismal class. More discipleship systems are needed; yet what is even more needed is personal relational coaching and mentoring by church leadership to make disciples (Matt 28:18). This key role of the leaders to mentor, not just teach, must be broadened beyond the pastor to empower even more mentors, teachers, and coaches of new and young believers. Is it possible people go out the backdoor because they are not mobilized for their ministry? Disciples can be trained through one-on-one discipleship, small life transformation groups, or cell groups for pastoral care, accountability, and spiritual growth. Many mature disciples who can coach and mentor are essential.

Aim for independent growth

Each disciple should be encouraged to grow, mature, and serve on their own and not be dependent on others, especially on clergy, to spiritually care for and feed them. To learn and grow, these believers need to cultivate inner disciplines through prayer, studying the Bible, and sharing their faith in word and deed. Disciples are not passive spectators in the church but active partners exercising their gifts in a God-given ministry. This is all enhanced by a caring circle of believers.

Develop a life-changing Christian community

To stimulate people in their faith, fight discouragement, and grow dependence on Jesus, each disciple needs a Christian community (Heb 10:24,25). Each growing believer contributes to their own spiritual renewal by active involvement in a community which in turn is renewing itself. Genuine relationships, deep discipleship, dynamic church life, and every believer participating in a valuable ministry will make it harder for disciples to leave the church by the backdoor.

Only a passionate gospel-centered spirituality based on meaningful relationships with a supportive structure can reverse these trends in making disciples in Japan. Some churches demonstrate this holistic discipleship where believers are growing, in ever-widening relationships, and ministering to others out of the grace in their life. This begins with the examples of church leaders. Most churches in Japan usually grow only by biological growth, often with only one baptism per year. Those churches with enthusiastic believers very naturally connect with non-believing Japanese in outreaches of evangelism and compassion. Whole disciples are more equipped to reach whole families and then transform whole communities. The gospel saves individuals, communities, and cultures (Jennings 2008, 44–45) and makes disciples and churches both stronger and holistic (Col 1:16).

PARTNER WITH OTHERS IN UNITY

Fifth, churches in Japan need to exhibit unity by partnering in significant ministry in their communities.

The Japanese church lacks deep unity and is reported as one of the most segregated churches in the world. Disunity in the church is sometimes fueled by a Japanese sense of overenthusiasm and loyalty for one's group over against other groups and loyalty to the King and his kingdom. Some of these issues are fed by Japanese collectivism where Japanese individuals place a high value on loyalty and honor of one's own group (Dale 1996, 19). As the typical local congregation in Japan is small (average thirty-five), many churches look inward and develop a fortress mentality. Most are not interested in cooperating and partnering with others outside their group or denomination.

Long-standing organization division continues between (1) several pre-war mainline denominations forced to merge by the Japanese government's Religious Bodies Law into the large *Kyōdan* denomination, (2) evangelicals often represented by the Japan Evangelical Association (JEA) formed in 1968 and re-formed in 1986, (3) charismatics often represented by the Nippon Revival Association (NRA) organized in 1996, and (4) The Japan Pentecostal Council established in 1998. Three groups have their own newspaper or magazine and three of them have formal membership based on their denominational affiliation (see Anderson 2013, 411; Hymes 2016, 167–68).

Often personal loyalties push any progress toward church unity farther away. Some individuals, churches, and denominations, pressured by government restrictions during the war years, compromised their Christian commitment. Some who did not compromise could resent others as a matter of spiritual pride. Over the years, unresolved personality issues and conflicts between individuals, leaders, and groups have undoubtedly developed. In some corners, there remains continued distrust, a competitive attitude, divisive and factional spirit (Gal 5:20), and lack of respect for other churches and ministries. In the long run, this undermines evangelism and kingdom advance.

Churches working together to sponsor a local ministry event is exemplary and happens regularly in Japan. These cooperative efforts need to continue as a first necessary step toward unity. However, the desire is not just to get along but to display the whole people of God in a community. We are admonished, based on the unity of the church, our faith, and the Godhead itself, to "make every effort to keep the unity of the Spirit through the bond of peace" (Eph 4:3). The biblical principles of handling personal conflict need to be consistently applied in the Japanese communal and hierarchical culture, no matter how difficult. Sins and trespasses need to be overlooked and forgiven. Reconciliation and forgiveness, which is not often biblically practiced in Japan, need to be validated by leaders, churches, and groups. Because we are one in Christ (Eph 4:4–6), we must all, at all times, be "completely humble and gentle; be patient, bearing with one another in love" (Eph 4:2).

Due to the small size of most congregations, churches need to partner with others for strength in numbers, mutual encouragement through teamwork, and a unified message to their non-believing communities. This is beyond their own group and their city to develop region-wide networks and alliances, not just for encouragement and fellowship but to exemplify true ministry partnership.

Unity should be sought for the right reasons and based on proper principles. What is needed is not unity for unity's sake, nor a desire to water down theological perspectives or historical uniqueness. Unity is not compromise of essential doctrine, nor is it putting major emphasis on minor doctrinal differences. Unity with mutual respect around Christ and championed by well-received agreements like the Lausanne Covenant have been essential. Unity is not based on comparison, conformity, or uniformity in ministry. Unity should be focused on shared vision and outcomes of ministry in communities. In this way, entire cities and regions can be engaged in ministry.

A few exemplary cases of local partnership exist for unified ministry based on mutual appreciation, openness, trust, and respect. For example, Sagamihara City, Kanagawa Prefecture is a large suburb of over 800,000 people in the Tokyo-Yokohama corridor. Here twenty-three churches partner together for shared youth ministry, a daycare center for the elderly, joint Bible school, and coordinated evangelism. Encouraged by the spirit and vision of a small number of pastors from that city, this partnership has continued for over forty years.

After the triple disaster of 2011, ministry in the Tohoku area underwent extreme transformation. Churches and groups that normally would not talk with each other were thrust together to meet the critical needs of disaster victims. This has fueled a new basis for partnering in ministry. Today the Miyagi Mission Network (MMN) helps foster ministry partnerships with churches and organizations throughout the whole of Miyagi Prefecture (see chapter four). This same spirit of partnering in unity has spread throughout the disaster area to include two other prefectures in a larger three-prefecture network.

But the church should not need a major natural disaster to understand the joint ministry that Christ has given the church. The unity of the church is to parallel the unity of the Godhead and a demonstration of that unity is a powerful witness to the work of Christ for all of us (John 17:20–22). This unity in mission can promote vision and stimulate engagement in mission in each church's local context.

RECOVER THE CHURCH'S MISSION

Sixth, churches in Japan need to move away from a fortress mentality to a mission mindset.

A typical characteristic of local churches in Japan is a protective and defensive posture. This posture continues the status quo and develops a survival disposition not unlike a fortress mentality. One example is worship services that are typically described as *reihai o mamori* (let us guard or observe worship). There is this static nature of the church in a protective mode instead of "doing church" or "being church."

The source of this fortress mentality is the influence of Japanese collectivism and the minority position of the church in Japan. Dale, who examined one of the fastest growing new religions in Japan, observed, "The church tends to stay too closed in upon itself; the 'old-timers' enjoy intimate fellowship among themselves, but do not reach out beyond the four walls of the church. They become an exclusive group of their own, according to the cultural pattern of group-centeredness" (Dale 1996, 16). Socially, the church becomes an ingrown clique. Mitani describes the church as *nakayoshi kurabu* (best buddy club), which is a key reason why the church cannot exceed 1 percent of the population (Mitani 2007, 9). Like many societies where group consensus and conformity are paramount, and where few whole families are Christ-followers, Christian believers sense incessant social pressure. Consequently, Japanese believers often develop an inferiority complex that reflects their stance in society.

Another source of this fortress mentality is a fixated adoration with Western cultural Christianity. Christianity introduced from Europe and North America carried over prevailing church views of the local parish, established clergy, and a preservation of ministry for a given community. Japan of the East, however, was completely unlike the church in the West where most people were content with the prevailing Christendom. In Japan, at most, Christianity was a minority religion in a moderately uninterested environment. Instead of a content status quo stance of Christendom, a more appropriate stance would be counter-cultural, developing a unique Japanese Christian culture.

The church exists for those not yet its members. The local church is not a club or society but the people of God as a spiritual community and family continually adopting new people into the faith. For the mission of the church in Japan, several correctives are suggested.

- The church needs to reverse its inward-looking directional orientation. The orientation needs to change from gathered to scattered, from attraction (come) to mission (send), from bringing people to church to bringing church to the community. Several churches throughout Japan have reversed their self-satisfied defensive stance to an outward missional mindset. One leader of a reproducing Japanese church described their mission philosophy: "We are not becoming busy inside the church but trying to do things outside . . . if we go out, there are plenty of places for ministry" (Mehn 2010, 112).

- Instead of being protective and defensive, the church has an offensive stance. Jesus said, "I will build my church and the gates of Hades will not prevail against it" (Matt 16:18). Jesus asserts that the church will be built despite the "gates of Hades." These gates are defensive, not offensive in nature. The church will advance, as the church that Christ builds will be offensive in destroying the Gates of Hades. Other metaphors of the church, like the church as the Building of God (Eph 2:20–21), imply unstoppable growth.

- The role of the church needs to move toward change and engagement. Japan has been described as a "tight culture" (Chan et al 1996, 1) because culture "imposes clear norms and reliably provides sanctions for deviation from norms" (Chan et al 1996, 2). So, change is not the norm and if change occurs in Japan, it occurs very slowly. The church must be an agent of change and fight against these cultural currents. Engagement must occur in local communities by proclaiming the word and accomplishing deeds of love. Because of Japan being a "tight culture," risk-taking, daring, and innovation are not encouraged (Chan et al. 1996, 5). Thus, to become more biblically consistent, the church must resist these tendencies with risk and engagement. The normally reactive church must be reversed to become proactive change agents engaged in its community. The church must look toward the possibilities of personal and societal transformation.

- Each local church needs to become a "bigger" church. Churches need to move beyond their own small local fellowship. Local churches were meant for interdependence. The minority and inferiority complexes can be overcome by celebrating and ministering with other believers. In some large ministry events, individual Christians are encouraged to know they are not alone and that there are many Christians like them. This can happen with associations, denominations, and networks. As already shared, churches need to do this locally and regionally as well. These kinds of kingdom connections should be primarily relational rather than organizational and for mutual encouragement and stimulation.

The often-small minority church must turn outward and from a defensive to a more offensive outlook. The purpose of the church is not stability and survival. The church is not meant to merely survive but to thrive on God, his gospel, and the multitude of promises to the church. The culture of Japan tends to seek harmony and stability, which is in sharp contrast to the biblical nature of the church. These changes in orientation and mindset will recover the mission of the church resulting in engagement in their communities; gospel transformation of individuals, churches, and communities; church health and growth; and the overall increase of disciples, leaders, and churches.

SUMMARY ON THE CHURCH

An overview of the existing church in Japan has been delineated. Some are encouraged about specific aspects of the existing church in Japan, but for others the overall evaluation is one of concern. In many places the church in Japan is declining and, overall, it is barely maintaining itself. We cannot come to any different conclusion than Braun observed over forty-five years ago. "Regardless of numerical attendance at worship and the size of the budget, a church which cannot bring into being new congregations of believers in nearby communities is spiritually poor" (Braun 1971, 93). Much revival and renewal of the church must occur so that the church will be healthy and growing.

This book is about reproducing and multiplying churches in Japanese soil through church planting movements. This means new churches and churches renewed and re-envisioned to carry out the task of the Great Commission. Bearing a holy dissatisfaction with the status quo, throughout this book we will address these challenges of responsiveness and meager church growth. After reflecting on some historical highpoints, later chapters will touch on effective models to reproduce churches (chapter five) and leadership for reproduction (chapter six). We will continually ask how we can revisit and rediscover the real strengths of the Japanese church.

Because of the disconnect of the church with the average Japanese, some leaders feel that a more radical approach is needed. They contend the far-reaching reformations required to bring the church to a healthy multiplying state will take too much time. For some this radical approach bypasses the existing churches and begins with fresh movements. Other leaders are more patient with intentional plans for the churches' renewal and change. Those with a more radical approach have advocated planting more relevant churches that will grow into movements. They encourage churches to give birth to new forms of the church rather than replicate the same structures that have already failed elsewhere. Church planting offers the opportunity to explore what it means for the church to become a genuinely missionary church with new responses to the challenges of a culture which has proved to be highly resistant to the message of the gospel. (Robinson and Christine 1992, 9)

Whatever your perspective on the condition of the existing church in Japan and what should be done, all of us should be unified in our understanding and our holy dissatisfaction with the condition of the church.

1. We should not despair and simply shift the blame to the culture and spiritual climate of Japan.
2. We must humbly admit the necessity of personal and corporate renewal of the church.
3. We must again affirm that the church is not called to simply react to culture but rather be an agent of cultural change.
4. We must assure that the church is healthy, growing, reproducing, and multiplying to fulfill Christ's Great Commission in Japan.
5. We all must ask what priorities and commitments are needed to bring revival and reformation to the existing church.
6. We must be hopeful and trust God for our shared goal.

We must remember God's intention for the church: "Now to him who is able to do immeasurably more than all we ask or imagine, according to his power that is at work within us, to him be glory in the church and in Christ Jesus throughout all generations, for ever and ever! Amen." (Eph 3:20–21).

THE GOSPEL PENETRATION IN JAPANESE SOIL

Doug Birdsall, former executive chair of the Lausanne Movement asserted, "There is no country in the world where the church has sown the gospel so generously, yet reaped so sparingly" (Foxwell-Barajas 2012, 17). We have seen much dedicated hard work but little gospel penetration in the soil of Japan. Many reasons could potentially be offered, but we considered just three broad reasons in these last two chapters. As the Japanese culture is so unique in the presentation of the gospel, we must consider a greater effort in contextualizing the gospel. Real spiritual resistance and warfare requires many prayer movements mobilized for Japan. Though we are grateful to God for the existing church, we recognize that this church must be revived and changed to become more missional and reproductive. These matters will be examined more in the chapters that follow.

In chapter three we will look at some historical snapshots of the church and glean some principles regarding ministry success as they relate to strategy and movements. Many of the issues discussed so far have been addressed by both past and present leaders. Some glimmers of hope from past and current leaders show how the church was rooted in Japan through key strategic thinking and practice.

JAPANESE RELIGIOUS MOVEMENTS

The purpose of this book is to explore the opportunities of multiplying churches in Japanese soil. The gospel as relevant in the Japanese context produces church health toward growing and multiplying churches. This chapter will look back into church and society from the Meiji Period (1868–1912) to the present. This will be a quick overview of some growing church movements and Christian approaches. Then we will look at some Japanese social and religious movements, both Christian and non-Christian, for their lessons correlated with multiplying churches.

INTRODUCTION

Throughout Japanese church history there have been many movements, ministries, and networks that have planted churches. As explained earlier, the church in Japan was introduced in the sixteenth century with the Roman Catholics. Following a long period of persecution and isolation, the country opened for a new surge in missionary work after 1859. From then Roman Catholics and Russian Orthodox churches along with several Protestant groups from North America and Europe entered and began planting the church. There was another surge in church planting after World War II.

We will take a look at this post-Meiji era planting of the church to gain insight in strategic principles in the establishment of churches and church planting movements. In returning to these very unique historic situations, we hope to stimulate new thinking and develop fresh insights and ideas for the planting of innovative churches in Japan. Lessons of history can be gleaned for application today. Later, current effective models of church planting and leadership will be explored, but we first want to look for some historical aspects of church planting in Japan.

INDIGENOUS CHURCH PLANTING BY NIKOLAI[2]

"The life and the life-fruits of Nicolai compel us to recognize him as one of the greatest missionaries of the modern era" (Drummond 1971, 354). He truly was a remarkable evangelist, church planter, and developer of leaders. "In sharp contrast to the slow growth of Protestant missions was the rapid growth of the Orthodox Church under the remarkable leadership of the Russian missionary, Nicolai" (Braun 1971, 117). Nikolai's winning of converts and development of Japanese leadership outstripped the combined Protestant and Catholic numbers over the same time period (Braun 1971, 117–118; Mullins 1998, 18; Kharin 2014, xi). At his death in 1912, his sixty-year accomplishments as a church planter were "two cathedrals, seven churches, 276 chapels, 175 meeting houses, thirty-four priests, eight deacons, 115 lay catechists, and 34,110 faithful" (Naganawa 2003, 122). Though today the Orthodox Church in Japan is not a very large group, there are many lessons we can learn from Nikolai's mission principles and practice.

First, he was dedicated to learning the language and culture of Japan. Traveling from St. Petersburg to his new consulate post in Hakodate in 1861, Nikolai Kasatkin was stranded due to winter weather and at that time met Bishop Innocent (Veniaminov), a returning veteran missionary to Alaska. Innocent compellingly encouraged Nikolai to study the Japanese language, history,

---

2. Transliterations of Ivan Dimitrovich Kasatkin's monastic name can be written as Nicolai or the more recently used Nikolai. We have chosen to use Nikolai when not used in quotations.

religion, and mores (Kharin 2014, 36). Nikolai took this challenge seriously and, benefiting from his position as chaplain in the Hakodate consulate, he intensely studied Japanese for eight years (Kharin 2014, 117). Throughout his ministry career he continued to learn, respect, and preserve the Japanese language and culture (Kharin 2014, 208–9). "His studies helped him not only to become proficient in Japanese but to gain the understanding of the people and their culture which enabled the Orthodox Mission to become quickly indigenized and to raise up Japanese leaders of distinction" (Drummond 1971, 341).

Second, he was committed to indigenous principles of church multiplication. Nikolai began with a strong commitment and practice of the Orthodox mission principle of indigenization of the church with little reliance on outside finances or workers (Naganawa 2003, 123–24). "There were never more than four foreigners in the work during the entire history of the Orthodox Church in Japan" (Stamoolis 1986, 36). To further the growth of local leadership and initiative, all missionaries "employed the incarnational approach" where they lived simply on the resources developed in ministry (Stamoolis 1986, 63).

From the beginning, Nikolai was prescient in realizing growing tensions between the governments of Russia and Japan; thus, he desired a separation from Russian political aims or entanglements. This lack of concern for his own country, Russia, was not common among most Orthodox workers, but he believed strongly in an indigenous Japanese church.

> Nicolai from the first intended that his church should be independent of the Church in Russia, and truly Japanese. To this end, he placed great emphasis upon preparing Japanese leadership, evangelization of Japan by the Japanese, the active participation of laymen and the administration of the Church. (Braun 1971, 117)

Third, he insisted on total mobilization of all believers for evangelism. Nikolai's plan to multiply the ministry based on local resources meant all converts were to be active in evangelism. This "enabled the gospel to be spread by the learned themselves without relying on extensive missionary support" (Stamoolis 1986, 36).

Fourth, he targeted whole families for evangelism. Nikolai saw that the Japanese family was essential to both win people to Christ and then continue to propagate the faith. He had a "distinctive view toward converting not just individuals but households" which "helped create family-based communities" (Kharin 2014, 38). These "self-propagating ecclesiastically-devoted households" would be the key to winning even more individuals and families (Kharin 2014, 208).

Fifth, he invested in developing strong national workers. Nikolai instituted a two-tiered training system where he conducted biweekly courses for teachers and leaders and weekly study circles for those seeking the faith. All training included studies in basic catechism including the Lord's Prayer and the Creed (Stamoolis 1984, 60).

> He introduced two kinds of leader. The congregations were in charge of the so-called "white priests," who received only minimum training. They conducted the liturgy in the churches. The overall work was ministered by the "black priests," men who are much more thoroughly trained. This flexible approach enabled Nicolai to multiply rapidly leaders who could give pastoral care. (Braun 1971, 117)

He developed an extensive use of lay catechists to conduct apostolic itinerant church planting, especially in rural areas where many endured much hostility (Naganawa 2003, 131). Nikolai also provided a system of seminary training for leaders which emphasized practical ministry. "Nicolai did not delay in ordaining Japanese as priests" (Drummond 1971, 344).

One would expect in the late nineteenth-century that the Orthodox Church as a high church would be comprised of a well-defined separation of clergy and laity. But in the Orthodox Church, the entire church, both the clergy and the laity, are guardians of the church's theology as the laity are actively involved in the governing councils of the Orthodox Church (Stamoolis 1986, 145n). As an evangelical Protestant, it is indeed sobering to consider that a nineteenth century leader of the Orthodox Church would more wholly exemplify the Protestant Reformation principle and practice of the priesthood of all believers than many Japanese Protestant churches commonly do.

Nikolai's ministry practice was informed not just by his theology but also by concrete realities of the Japanese context. This led to effective evangelism, developing indigenous churches and leaders.

He was a great disciple and mentor of others, and among "all the foreign Christian evangelists who worked in Japan during the early modern era, only Archbishop Nikolai nurtured so many direct disciples" (Naganawa 2003, 124). But after Nikolai passed from the scene in 1912, the fruitfulness he demonstrated could not be continually cultivated through ongoing growth and reproduction toward even more leaders and churches; the Orthodox Church in Japan slowly declined (Braun 1971, 117–18).

THE JAPAN HOLINESS CHURCH

The Holiness Church developed from the evangelistic work of the Oriental Missionary Society led by Mr. and Mrs. Charles Cowman and Juji Nakada. The mission society that was originally non-denominational later formed the Japan Holiness Church in 1917 (Yamamori 1974, 118). This church underwent momentous growth, going from 1,600 members in 1917 to 19,523 members in 1932 with forty-six churches and sixty-four pastors (ibid., 116,130). The growth of the Holiness Church on its own outstripped the combined growth of the first early five Protestant denominations, which by itself was respectable.

Tetsunao Yamamori in his book *Church Growth in Japan* lists the reasons for this rapid growth of the Japan Holiness Church.

1. The church "utilized the existing social structure advantageously by emphasizing the conversion of the whole family as a unit" (130). Yamamori maintains that the Holiness group decided on a different kind of evangelism focused on non-believers and not church activities. He explains that

   > the conversion approach has been defined as the experiential and group-oriented way into the church. The convert had a radical religious experience and could not contain within himself the joy of salvation. He shared the good news with his family, relatives, and friends. In this way, the essentially individualist response to the faith often triggered group response. Sometimes, whole families and people and groups join the church together. (128)

2. New converts were immediately trained and mobilized to share their faith with others.

3. Meetings anticipated and included revivals that "deepened the spiritual life of the whole church and heightened its evangelistic zeal" (131).

4. There was vision to reach unevangelized remote regions with the gospel. However, "when faced with the solid wall of irresponsiveness, it shifted its emphasis to the more receptive populations in the city" (132).

5. The church "had a multiple leadership structure" (132) of both clergy and lay people for evangelism

and church planting. Clergy were accepted with the most basic qualifications and "the laity took seriously the doctrine of the priesthood of all believers" (132). And the church was "most successful in mobilizing its laity. The spirit filled artisan could become a leader of a churchlet (a small cell group meeting in a home), and this pattern was reproducible" (132).

6. The church "was most equipped to reach the masses and actually receive its strongest support from them. . . . it gathered within its membership blue-collar workers, employers and employees of small business concerns and their dependents" (132–33).

7. "Nakada through his charismatic leadership challenged the entire Holiness constituency with high goals of attainment. . . . he stated . . . the advance depended on its evangelism-centered policy" and one time challenged them to win one million souls to Christ (133).

After this period of rapid conversion and church growth there was a period of decline due to a major split in the organization and then later religious persecution. Due to Juji Nakada's changing eschatological views, especially related to the role of the Jewish people, the church underwent an organizational split resulting in two groups in 1936 (Mullins 1998, 105; Ikegami 2003, 132). In 1942, during a period of government control of religion, over one hundred pastors of the Holiness Church were arrested and many churches were closed. These leaders were later tried and sentenced to prison where several leaders died (Drummond 1971, 268). The Holiness group never again recovered this exemplary growth.

EARLY CHURCH GROWTH STUDY BY YAMAMORI

Tetsunao Yamamori conducted a detailed study of eight Christian denominations from the Meiji period to the beginning of

World War II (1859–1939). His study compared denominations that expanded rapidly and others that grew more slowly with the same historical, social, and cultural conditions and over the same time period. He concluded that there were striking differences, "a gulf" as he described it, in the methodology of those groups that expanded churches and those that experienced slower growth (Yamamori 1974, 104–8).

1. Those denominations that were able to mobilize more leaders, such as missionaries at the beginning and national workers later, experienced faster growth.
2. Those groups that had a more highly trained leadership were more flexible and competent to reach people in society.
3. Denominations that had more churches and also made more contact with people in society experienced faster growth.
4. Growing denominations had more comprehensive plans for evangelism, meaning more energy was devoted to effective methods than experimenting with unproven approaches.
5. Those denominations that were capable of touching the segments in Japanese society that were more receptive—at that time students and intellectuals—experienced greater growth.
6. Growing denominations passed on to national leaders the responsibility for evangelism and the DNA for church multiplication.

INDIGENOUS JAPANESE CHRISTIAN MOVEMENTS

Many principles of church development can be learned from indigenous Japanese Christian movements. Until the 1998 publication of Mark Mullins's book *Christianity Made in Japan: A Study of Indigenous Movements,* very little was researched or written on these movements. His research of the sociology of religion examines thirteen independent Christian movements indigenous to Japan which started from 1901 through 1977. He defines indigenous in the classic way of nineteenth-century mission leaders Henry Venn and Rufus Anderson as self-supporting, self-governing, and self-propagating (Mullins 2003, 126–27). Beginning with Kanzo Uchimura and the Non-Church Movement, Mullins highlights the growth, development, teachings, and leadership of each of these various movements. He sees these indigenous movements not unlike Christian versions of the New Religions which have sprung up in many quarters of Japan. They "at least share in common the conviction that God is calling them to develop Japanese cultural expressions of the Christian faith that are at least as legitimate as the national churches and denominational forms that have emerged over the centuries in Europe and North America" (Mullins 1998, 28).

Regarding church multiplication in Japanese soil, one useful example of the sociological principles of these indigenous movements is the Spirit of Jesus Church, officially known by its Japanese name *Iesu no Mitama Kyōkai*. This church group "is an entirely indigenous body which receives no aid in finances or personnel from abroad" (Drummond 1971, 283), which has grown rapidly since World War II from 436 in 1948 to 433,108 adherents in 1993. With over two hundred churches and over four hundred evangelistic house churches (Braun 1971, 172; Mullins 1998, 163)[3] it became one of the largest Protestant denominations in Japan and "now is the largest Pentecostal denomination in Japan" (Anderson 2013, 154). Braun compares The Spirit of Jesus Church's rapid growth to churches in Korea and Brazil (Braun 1971, 172), stating

---

3. This religious organization handles statistics a bit differently than other churches. The numbers indicate the number of those who have come to faith and not necessarily regular attendees. As a principle, the church probably has an active membership of one percent of the number of adherents (Trevor 1993, 21). The church officially reports "active membership" as 23,283. (Mullins 1998, 164).

that it "has managed to establish more churches across Japan than any other indigenous movement" (Mullins 1998, 102).

This group was founded by Jun Murai, the son of a Methodist minister who attended Aoyama Gakuin in Tokyo. At one point, contemplating suicide, he had a religious experience of the Holy Spirit. Leaving his studies, he began to do evangelistic work and assumed a pastorate in Tokyo. In 1941, he visited the True Jesus Church in Taiwan when he decided to resign his church in Tokyo. While they were there, his wife reported seeing a revelation from God about organizing a new church.

This church movement confesses that it is a Christian church. Due to the influence of Pentecostal "oneness" theology, it believes in the deity of Christ but rejects the Trinity. Murai and other followers have attempted to address issues of Japanese folk religion and issues of the dead, so the church practices the ritual of vicarious baptism for the dead (Braun 1971, 173). The belief that it is the only true church defines it as a sect. Mullins feels that this movement is "best understood as an indigenous Christian sect" (1990, 370). Others would consider it to have serious doctrinal error for the above beliefs and practices (Hymes 2016, 171–72).

Mullins feels that the glory days of this movement are over (1998, 164); however, several principles are helpful in understanding how to multiply churches in Japanese soil.

- Focus on the practicality of religion and religious experiences—in order to achieve this practicality, the church rejects intellectualism (Mullins 1998, 101; cf. Nagasawa 2002, 62).
- Emphasizes families and household—the household system of "social organization and leadership succession has a long history in Japan" (Mullins 1998, 187). In many cases the church has grown well by reaching whole households and developing leadership of the church along kinship lines (ibid., 103).

- Mobilization for evangelism—the whole church, both laity and clergy, is mobilized for evangelism (Braun 1971, 132).
- Financial independence—"Its leaders receive no monetary aid, either for their education or for their efforts at church planting" (ibid., 173).
- Simple organization—the church "is a streamlined religious organization with no committees or bureaucracy" (Mullins 1998, 103) and uses home meetings (Braun 1971, 173).

NEW RELIGIONS IN JAPAN

Beginning in Japan's Meiji period, a second wave during the 1920s, and then exploding due to the religious freedom after World War II, hundreds of *shin shūkyō* (new religions) rushed to the scene, building on the old religious core of Shintoism, Buddhism, and Confucianism (McFarland 1967; Earhart 2014, 228). "In spite of the great variety of their doctrines, new religions share unity of aspiration and worldview significantly different from those of secular society and from the so-called established religions" (Hardacre 1986, 3). These new religions exploded by meeting the "concrete worries and concerns in people's daily lives" (Shimazono 2003, 280). They tapped into some of the concerns of rural people moving to the city and some of the more modern elements of frustration in the Japanese society. New religions are a remarkable social phenomenon in the history of Japan and are "unquestionably the largest and fastest-growing popular movement" (Garon 1986, 273). Between 10 and 20 percent of Japanese are estimated to be members of one of the new religions (Prohl 2012, 241).

This "success" in tapping into the inner needs of society far outpaces the commitment, investment, and hard work by the Christian church. Just one of these new religions, Soka Gakkai, in the 1950s "could develop a membership larger than the total number of all Christians (Catholic, Protestant, and

Orthodox combined) after almost a century of intense missionary efforts" (Earhart 2014, 274).

New religions make subtle breaks from the established religions of Japan. Where established religions have a long tradition of shrines and temples, some new religions downplay or do not even possess these sacred places. Established religions are led by a well-organized system of clergy; many new religions place a strong emphasis on lay involvement. These two factors have propelled new religions into modern urbanized Japan. This is "in contrast to a tendency of the older faiths to be impersonal, clerical, academic, and tradition-written, these new religions have a way of making ordinary people believe that they are concerned about them and their problems individually, and have a technique, and a fellowship, that can help." (Ellwood 2008, 210).

New religions emphasize spiritual healing and providing solutions for family and emotional problems (ibid.). Because of this emphasis on personal matters, in contrast to the household (*ie*) faith, "one hallmark of New Religions is that they made a more direct appeal to individual faith" (Earhart 2004, 189). Unlike the established religions customarily based on one's kinship or geographical area, the new religions developed in urbanized Japan are voluntary organizations (ibid., 225) and very adaptive and syncretistic. These characteristics of new religions has prompted Earhart to make the conclusion that "these religious movements are as much renovation as innovation, as much renewed religious traditions as new traditions" (ibid., 187).

From the dozens of new religious movements, we want to survey two of the fastest growing groups, Soka Gakkai and Rissho Koseikai, which have been researched for insights into the Japanese religious climate and for lessons for growing the Christian church in Japan.

Soka Gakkai

Founded in 1930 by recent convert, Tsunesaburo Makiguchi, as Soka Gakkai (Value Creation Society) out of the "extreme" Nichiren Shōshū Buddhism (Ellwood 2008, 200). The group holds central the Lotus Sutra as the only authoritative truth and as the one true Buddhism for the world. Later laymen Josei Toda and Daisaku Ikeda led this Buddhist lay group. It developed in urban areas and spread into rural villages. Soka Gakkai today has 12 million adherents in Japan (Prohl 2012, 244) and 1.5 million overseas (Ellwood 2008, 204). In 1964, Soka Gakkai formed its own political party *Kōmeitō* (Clean Government Party). The group's fast growth has since leveled out. In 1991, there was a contentious split from the priestly led Nichiren Shōshū Buddhist organization.

Soka Gakkai was highly mobilized in local neighborhoods where members participated in group activities and helping others (ibid., 202). Their membership was very organized as every family belonged to a local "unit" and a larger "block." All members were mobilized for propagation and new members were "required to be active in proselytizing others" (Earhart 2014, 243). Yamamori in his study of Japanese church growth attributes Soka Gakkai's phenomenal growth "to the creation of aggressive evangelistic fervor among the members" (Yamamori 1974, 147). Propagation, training, and encouragement of all members was conducted in the local small groups called *zadankai*. Soka Gakkai's "distinctive emphasis has been on perfection of the individual through group counseling circles where leaders give guidance on personal problems in the light of sutra teaching" (Reid 1991, 29). These groups reinforce doctrine, evangelistic intensity, and engagement with their communities.

Rissho Koseikai

Founded in 1938 by Nikkyo Niwano, Rissho Koseikai, or Society Establishing Righteousness and Harmony, is a breakoff movement from Reiyuaki, another new religion. Like Soka Gakkai, this organization is part of Nichiren Buddhism and believes in the authoritative truth of the Lotus Sutra (Ellwood 2008, 204). The group utilizes small groups called *Hoza*, often called "the circle of harmony," where members advise and counsel one another and new prospects can learn of the group's message. There are currently 6 million members of this new religion (Prohl 2012, 245).

NEW NEW RELIGIONS OF JAPAN

In the 1970s and 80s other new religions arose without ties to established Japanese religious traditions. These New New Religions *(shin shinshūkyō)* are more aligned with the worldwide "New Age" movement, other spirituality, and streams of Buddhism previously uncommon in Japan, such as Vajrayana (or esoteric) Buddhism and Tibetan Buddhism. These new religions have not shown the rapidly growing social movements of the new religions after World War II, and many commercialize on religious goods and services (Prohl 2012, 242). Some examples of these groups are Agonshu (Agama School), Mahikari (True Light), and Kofuku no Kagaku (Science of Happiness). One of the widest known is Aum Shinrikyo (Supreme Truth) which perpetrated the sarin nerve gas attack on the Tokyo subways in March 1995. This organization changed its name to Aleph in 2000, and Hikari no Wa (The Circle of Rainbow Light) split off in 2007.

SOME KEY LESSONS

Several principles are helpful in understanding how religious movements advance.

Sharing a Relevant Message

The group's message focuses on practical living and they are more "concerned about personal problems than about abstract questions of principle and authority" (Reid 1991, 28). As stated earlier, they present religion as having *genze riyaku* or "practical bene-fits in this lifetime" (Reader & Tanabe 1998, 2). The message is also personal. "The principal reason that people join new religious organizations of this type is to find help with health, marital, financial, and other problems" (Reid 1991, 29).

Utilization of Small Groups

Small groups are used as an entry point for conversions. "Most nonmembers made their first contact with Soka Gakkai when a member who happened to be a friend, relative, or coworker persuaded them to attend a meeting" (Earhart 2014, 202). These groups are small, meet in homes, are informal, and are usually based on discussion employed for conversions, membership, and community. "All the new religions, however, provide their partic-ipants with a tightly organized, protective community, with study groups and social activities that minister perhaps more to their social than their spiritual needs" (Reischauer 1988, 215; cf. Dale 1975, 65). Small groups are used to prevent membership leakage (Yamamori 1974, 151).

Multi-level Leadership

All religious movements are dependent on leadership for propa-gation, for the development of organization, and for reproduction and multiplication. These groups have outstanding leadership, a clear cause, and means for developing leadership within the move-ment (Hesselgrave 1978a, 308–322). These leaders cast vision and gain ownership for goals in the growth of their organizations.

Mobilization of the Laity for Propagation

"The whole organization is geared to enlist every member in the program of propagation of the faith" (Hesselgrave 1978b, 139). The primary means of propagation is "personal enthusiasm and testimony more than theological arguments" (Elwood 2010, 210). The mobilization of laity can also be seen in the Christian cults of the Mormons and Jehovah's Witnesses. Not only are they mobilized, but they are regularly "out there" touching lives and meeting people.

CONCLUSION

One of the purposes of this book is to understand the Japanese context more completely in order to be more effective in planting churches in Japanese soil. To learn from the past, this chapter took a cursory look as far back as the Meiji period at the church and society. Researcher Yamamori's advice is still relevant for us today "The causes for each of the situations must be scrutinized by church historians and missionary scholars who are well-versed in the activities of the church during this period" (Yamamori 1974, 113). More research would be very beneficial.

We considered some situations causing rapid growth of the church. We also looked at the sociological phenomena of religious movements in Japan, both Christian and non-Christian, to discover biblical and sociological principles for multiplying the church in Japan. These movements follow the social structure of Japan and reach whole families. Their leaders develop dreams and goals for growth; cultivate multi-level leadership, not just professional clergy; and commend a pivotal role for the laity. Everyone is mobilized for the propagation of their beliefs. As indigenous movements, they engage the culture, beliefs, and worldview of Japan. In the next chapter, we will survey some church strategies related to church planting in Japan.

4

STRATEGIC PERSPECTIVES ON CHURCH PLANTING

This chapter will consider some post-war strategic ideas and their implementation in Japan that fostered church planting advance. As there is very little written on church planting ministry in Japan, this chapter will outline several networks, effective ministries, and current trends shaping church planting multiplication. We will also touch on natural disasters and their effect on the church and gospel ministry.

POST-WAR APOSTOLIC MISSIONARIES

Joseph Meeko and Ralph Cox were among the first generation of missionaries after World War II. Ralph Cox's ministry that spanned over fifty years was primarily focused on church planting in Kagawa prefecture on the island of Shikoku. Joseph Meeko worked for just twelve years in Yamagata Prefecture in the Tohoku region, as well as the Kanto area (later he returned for seven additional years). Meeko, with the help of others, started at least twelve Japanese churches in five years, and Ralph started at least eighty-eight churches.[4] They are two well-known examples of their generation.

Both shared the intense commitment of establishing local churches. These two pioneers took the apostolic role of founding and birthing churches. Often, they were the first missionaries to visit a rural village. They prioritized evangelism, making disciples, and leaders. Cox and Meeko did both this pioneer church

---

4. For a longer article on these two missionaries see Mehn 2014, 24–26.

planting work and church planting facilitating through others. They were successful in casting vision and developing systems of church multiplication. Even though they are from a different era of Japanese missions, we can learn much from their underlying ministry principles and practices.

- Cultivate God-sized vision: They thought big but worked small. They loved to show potential leaders big vistas and engage them in big plans.
- Create emergent opportunities: Meeko was a great proponent of what he called "strawberry evangelism"— starting another church before the first church plant is fully ripened. Cox advocated starting more than one church plant at the same time. They believed more in multiple opportunities than in optimum situations.
- Mobilize lay people for ministry: They believed in planting the types of churches where lay people could be actively involved in leadership. Cox outlined New Testament principles so that church planting could be done by non-professionals and over a wide area. They often used local workers and raised up harvest workers from the harvest. Meeko's early church plants used teams of people, including seminary students and veteran pastors. As it was not practical to wait for highly trained and credentialed professional clergy, both of them entrusted ownership of the ministry to lay people and taught lay leaders ministry lessons through on-the-job training.
- Invest in people: They saw their role as equippers of leaders, discipling and training many. They counselled and advised many pastors and lay leaders. Ralph engaged with the then-new concept of short-term missionaries.

These post-war missionaries show us that certain ministry principles were effective in reproducing the church in Japan.

Their exact methods may not be reproducible today, but we can still learn many principles from their church planting ministries.

POLITY FOR SATURATION

During the Meiji Era foreigners and missionaries were restricted to a few ports of entry so churches were first developed in Nagasaki, Kobe, Yokohama, Hakodate, and a few other places. Due to the government restriction on conversion, rescinded in 1873, most mission activity was centered on education and medical ministry. Ministry was focused on these ports and later into other areas.

After World War II, especially with the large influx of new missionaries, conscious effort was made to develop polity agreements between church denominations and mission agencies to provide saturation of churches throughout Japan. Many groups continued to work in their initial starting point of the major cities of the island of Honshu and especially the Kanto area, but then later sent out workers to more remote areas. That is why many Japanese denominations throughout Japan today are only located in certain regions. Later, as their members were transferred for school or work, some denominations established churches in areas outside their initial church planting mission field. Some of the larger denominations with greater resources envisioned having a more national impact for their church planting. The Southern Baptists worked at developing a strong central church in each prefectural capital that would permeate that prefecture and beyond.

After the war, in order to track where new churches were being planted and to avoid unnecessary ministry duplication, Church Information Service (CIS) was developed by the Japan Evangelical Missionary Association's (JEMA) church planting arm. This service would assist missionaries, and later Japanese, in finding unchurched areas with demographic information and maps of existing churches. Several years later, CIS left JEMA to become independent and serve the whole church in Japan with their research and databases. In 2014, CIS merged with the recently developed Faith and Work department of Tokyo Christian University, now called Japan Missions Research (JMR).

About this same time a new network emerged for people focused on reaching the over 1,800 unreached rural areas of Japan. The Japan Rural Church Planting Network (RJCPN), launched by missionaries, conducts seminars and training for people serving in rural areas and also urban churches wishing to extend ministry into nearby rural areas. They continue to update data for church planting through an internet online database and mapping of all unreached rural areas for saturation.

PIONEER CHURCH PLANTING

Most of the early churches in Japan were started by missionary church planters. When they were available, Japanese national partners worked together with missionaries to establish churches, especially after World War II. Once these churches were strong enough, the missionary would withdraw to start another church in another location. If there was a Japanese worker, they remained behind to lead the newly established church. It was unusual for the Japanese worker to also leave to go somewhere else and develop another church. The smooth transfer of leadership in these pioneer churches from a missionary to a Japanese brings some uncertainties. Even though many patterns of passing the leadership baton were used, many churches declined after these transitions.

Later, as small groups of established churches were founded, they took the initiative to further expand their churches throughout their regions. Regional districts of churches could then recruit a church planter and supply the funding for a new church. This occurred on the national level as well. National denominations wanting to establish new churches in a completely new area recruited, coached, and supported these workers. For many years, the vision and support for church planting often came from a national or regional organization.

This procedure was followed: planting the church through the pioneer church planting pattern, sometimes with or without regional church planting support. After many years of this practice, resulting in many established churches, new options and approaches in starting churches have arisen.

Since the late 1980s there has been a large uptick in independent churches—many having an average worship attendance over a hundred. Many of these churches that did not belong to a denomination or network have a vision for planting churches. Some of these churches developed into new independent churches.

Other churches developed their own network of churches. For example, the Tokyo Horizon Chapel in Machida, Tokyo was an independent church. Due to a vision for evangelism and ministry, this church has its own network of seven churches. The Keisen Network of churches is a result of a Conservative Baptist church in Yamagata prefecture planting over twenty churches throughout Japan. Many churches could be started simply with a healthy mother church spawning daughter and even granddaughter churches.

In the early 1990s many church planting missionaries in Japan, with the influence of the cell church movement and writings by David Garrison and others, began to see the potential for going beyond planting churches to catalyzing movements. To foster Church Planting Movements (CPM) many of these workers focused on facilitating church planting by raising up Japanese workers or Japanese catalysts. Most of these churches were based on simple church networks or cell church reproduction, which will be discussed in chapter five.

CHURCHES PLANTING MOVEMENTS

About this same time many healthy churches and networks outside of Japan developed a vision for planting churches in Japan. These churches went about planting the church in Japan in a similar pattern as in their home country. They would select a church planter, form a church planting team, send the team to Japan, and establish the first church as a beachhead for church multiplication throughout Japan. These key Japanese churches would be the basis to launch multiple movements within Japan and beyond. Here are a few examples:

- New Hope Oahu, Hawaii (Pastor Wayne Cordeiro) sent workers who planted the first church in Tokyo, which has planted churches in Yokohama, Osaka, Narimasu (Tokyo), Gifu, and Taiwan.
- A Nigerian church denomination has sent missionaries to establish a base in Japan for many churches.
- Hope Chapel Honolulu, Hawaii (Pastor Ralph Moore) with their global network of over one thousand churches established several churches in Okinawa, Nishinomiya, and the Tokyo area.
- Redeemer Presbyterian Church in Manhattan New York (Pastor Tim Keller) with a vision to establish transformational churches in key global centers through their City to City initiative launched their first church plant in Tokyo in 2009. The Tokyo network now has a network of four churches (see chapter five).
- Many other churches from several nations have established churches in Japan to launch multiplying networks.

LAY CHURCH PLANTING

Lay people have always planted churches in Japan, but in recent years there has been a growing interest in intentionally mobilizing lay people as a strategy in planting churches. Due to the influence of church planting networks and simple church strategies of house and cell churches, some local churches, church networks, and mission agencies have been encouraging lay involvement in planting churches.

Below are some examples of the variety of lay church planting approaches and situations.

1. A local school teacher saw a need for his community and started a church in his home. He continues to pastor this new church and work as a teacher. His ministry leadership is supported by several people in his network.

2. A medical doctor and his wife gather people weekly to meet at their medical clinic.

3. A church member has a burden to reach out and have a healthy church. She prays that God would send others to join her. God honors that prayer and she goes to her church leadership who bless her in starting meetings in her home.

4. A lay person desires to start a home church in his community. He gathers a small group of people for worship and Bible study in a local church building of another group.

5. A pastor is coaching one of his lay people to form a chapel from the mother church. He and his wife have a worship service as an evangelistic outreach for his community in their home. Those attending, apart from this couple, are not connected with the mother church. The mother church pastor meets with him monthly for fellowship and ministry coaching.

6. An established church sends out a team of about ten lay people to establish a bilingual church in another community. The church develops to an average attendance of over two hundred.

7. A businessman gathers a group of people in a rental space of a building near a downtown train station.

8. A middle-aged couple was transferred to another city for work. They built their home specifically with a larger meeting room in mind for worship services.

The wife, as a gifted evangelist, won several people to Christ. They gathered for formal worship services in their home. Later their son graduated from seminary and assumed the role of pastor of this church in their own facility.

9. A doctor was instrumental in leading a group of people in the hospital to Christ. They meet weekly at the hospital for fellowship towards winning more to Christ.

Some frequent patterns in these lay churches:[5]

- They are led by lay people who are not clergy by vocation, but several have some theological training and many have volunteered at their church part-time.
- These churches are primarily simple churches (house churches) meeting in homes or other suitable places.
- They are predominantly a small group of people (usually less than twenty).
- The church often develops in one of three ways: 1) winning several people to Christ through direct evangelism, 2) discontent with the church situation in Japan and wanting to do more in ministry, or 3) a group of people gathering and needing some leadership.

Some common elements with lay church planters:

- They have had some exposure to church planting through training, a seminar, their local church, or talking to others doing church planting. This exposure stimulated them, developed a "holy discontent," and ignited a vision for not just planting a church, but launching a movement of church planting.

---

5. CPI established a research project to determine how best to understand and support lay people planting churches. Unfortunately, there was not enough response for in-depth research. What is included here is some of the data collected with broad overviews.

- They pray to God about this burden for new churches and for others to join them.
- Some have outside support from a mentor, their home church, or a network.

Some suggestions gained from observations of these lay-led churches:

- If more lay people are exposed to church planting principles, more may be interested in starting a church. More people need to be challenged and given permission to plant churches.
- There seems to be little training and skill development available for lay people starting churches. Simple basic training needs to be developed with them in mind.
- Those that have personal support and coaching take advantage of it. Others do not have it. More support needs to be developed for lay church planters.
- It is helpful when a lay church planter belongs to a network for encouragement, training, and support.

INTERNATIONAL VIP CLUB

The International VIP Club was started in 1993 by a group of businessmen desiring to evangelize and disciple business people, especially men. Few businessmen attend churches due to their very busy schedule and their "marriage to the company." After some initial club meetings, the VIP club sponsored some evangelistic meetings in downtown hotels with large numbers in attendance—in one case over 450 people. These were all led by lay Christian businessmen. Participants were then encouraged to launch their own clubs in their areas. Many of them gathered in meeting rooms, hotel restaurants, offices, participants' homes, or any place that was convenient from their place of business. These local groups also sponsored evangelistic meetings to reach more businessmen. The number of clubs has expanded to hundreds throughout cities in Japan and internationally.

The VIP clubs continue to be active and are ministering to business people effectively by reaching men who are often difficult for the church to reach. Yet as these businessmen are meeting near their place of business rather than the communities where they live, there is a disconnect with local churches. VIP clubs insist they are parachurch organizations and are not engaged with or acting as local churches. The leadership of VIP clubs continues to be Christian business people and very few clergy are involved. Some local churches host these clubs, but as of yet the expansion into new churches has not occurred. Mitsuo Fukuda has expressed concern that local churches should not interfere, but instead allow VIP clubs freedom to develop as a movement normally (Fukuda 2000, 96–97). It is hoped that some simple churches would result from this lay movement.

THE APPEARANCE OF MINISTRY NETWORKS

In the late 1980s and early 1990s there were several ministries and networks across denominational lines that encouraged and trained in church health and church planting.

The Japan Church Growth Institute (JCGI) was organized by Life Ministries (later renamed Asian Access) to provide a two-year special study program with personal coaching for pastoral leaders desiring their churches to grow. Besides internal church growth and health, church reproduction and multiplication were emphasized. At the end of their two-year program, pastors were assigned to design and present to their cohort a church growth plan. Many of these plans included large-scale church planting plans. For example, Pastor Hiroyuki Akae of the Saidaiji church in Okayama Prefecture, designed the Seto Inland Sea Plan which included planting strategic churches affiliated with his denomination throughout the region. At least seven of these churches have been planted (Akae 1997). Many of these JCGI graduates exemplify leadership for church health and continue leading their churches in growth and reproduction.

In 1996, through JCGI, Japan's first Church Planting Network was inaugurated in Yamagata prefecture under the mentorship of Robert Logan. After three years, the five churches in that network had reproduced five new churches. Pastor Jiro Chida, one of the original network pastors, is often quoted as saying that it is hard for one church to start another church, but it is very easy for three churches to start one church. Since 1996, JCGI has established nearly thirty networks in many regions and prefectures of Japan resulting in the planting of over 160 churches. The actual design and implementation of this church planting model will be discussed in chapter five.

Church planting networks were first developed and implemented in North America. Since then, other countries, like Japan, have adapted them for their contextual situation. Generally, the recommendation from successful network practitioners is to recruit all the churches in the network as part of the same denomination. However, nearly the opposite has occurred in Japan, where it is more common for all the churches in the network to come from various denominations. The larger kingdom vision and the need for mutual help in church reproduction have been more powerful than the normal tendency for churches to stay within their church family. Each of these networks also reveals the motivation to develop a new task group committed to church reproduction and multiplication.

Another network of leaders and churches was developed to emphasize the need for discipling believers in local churches. The *Shoboku-sha* network or, in English, "Little Shepherds" network believed in the one Great Shepherd Jesus as the leader of the church; anyone else, including clergy and laity, were just "little shepherds." This emphasis addressed some of the clergy-laity gap and mobilized many lay people in discipleship and church leadership. This network of churches provided direct lay training to disciple others alongside pastoral training to disciple the laity and to multiply disciples in their own congregations.

Beginning with a base of some Korean churches, this network became a national movement that developed and published many discipleship materials and conducted training events throughout Japan. After the resignation of one of the movement's key leaders due to scandal, this network has nearly disappeared.

After a visit to Japan by Ralph Neighbor, a key proponent of the cell church model of churches, there was increased interest in the cell church model to help typical Japanese churches become multipliers of disciples, small groups (cells), and new churches. Later a connection was made with Hong Kong cell church pastor Ben Wong that helped this Japanese group form the Japan Cell Church Mission Network (JCMN). This group has networked about 150 churches throughout Japan that are committed to healthy church principles and developing lay leadership, cell groups, and planting cell churches. Their vision, as revealed by their name, also includes world mission engagement. This network has developed curriculum for cell church ministry and conducts seminars and conferences throughout Japan. Lately it has developed at least ten regional pastor-coaching networks to develop pastoral and lay leadership for growth, reproduction, and mission (more on coaching below).

In 1994, a small group of missionaries to Japan gathered for a church planting seminar near Mount Fuji, under the sponsorship of the Japan Evangelical Missionary Association (JEMA). From that first event many workers have enlarged their vision for church planting movements from the Church Planting Institute (CPI) vision statement, "Advancing God's kingdom by mentoring leaders who are a part of a movement that are multiplying churches that are multiplying disciples through the power of the gospel." Today CPI has trained over three thousand leaders from over two hundred mission agencies and denominations from every region of Japan in church planting and spiritual renewal principles. Trainers from overseas, missionaries to Japan, and national pastors regularly conduct regional training in evangelism, discipleship, leadership development, and church multiplication. Biennial CPI national conferences—sometimes topping five hundred in attendance—provide training, renewal, and inspiration for the dream of Japan filled with healthy transformational churches that are multiplying in Japan and throughout the world. Though this organization continues to be mission-led under JEMA, large numbers of the participants are Japanese pastors and workers.

In 1998 Rick Warren's *Purpose Driven Church* was published in Japan under the title "Keys to a Healthy Church." This led to a growing interest in the Purpose Driven church model and Purpose Driven church planting in Japan. Some materials were translated into Japanese and distributed throughout Japan. More recently several leaders reorganized the group as Purpose Driven Church (PDC) Japan, publishing training materials and conducting seminars for churches wanting to implement the PDC model. While it is characterized by an emphasis on evangelism, discipling, and developing leaders, this group in Japan has not yet emphasized the original vision of Rick Warren and the Saddleback Community Church for establishing and multiplying churches.

The appearance of these parachurch and interdenominational networks seem to reveal that local churches and denominations have not provided the types of training and networking that Japanese leaders feel is necessary to grow healthy disciples, leaders, and new churches. Many of these networks such as JCGI, CPI, JCMN, PDC, and others continue to train leaders and workers, provide interdenominational encouragement and cross-fertilization of ideas, and raise more vision for church planting throughout Japan. These types of networks will need to increase and expand if local churches and leaders will be adequately supported and trained.

COACHING FOR LEADERSHIP DEVELOPMENT

Coaching skills for developing leaders became very popular in the 1990s especially in business contexts. Today coaching systems are widely used in Japan for business leaders and in life coaching. Coaching as a development tool for church leadership is still relatively unknown and hence not practiced by most Japanese pastors. Traditionally, most Japanese church leaders were to conform to their group and follow the advice of their senior leaders.

As mentioned above, JCGI has a church growth cohort for pastors in addition to regional church planting networks to develop leaders. In both of these training programs, JCGI feels coaching is a central tool to develop leaders. Besides their regular group meetings for prayer, training, and encouragement, all leaders are assigned a personal coach for two or three years.

Previously, the concept of coaching others in the Japan context was often seen as top-down teaching and advising, often directive, and sometimes even abusive. Therefore, JCGI has redefined the word "coaching" as "Barnabas Ministry." The focus is to be like Barnabas (cf. Acts 4:36–37; 9:26–28; 11:21–26) and be an encourager by simply coming alongside to assist and equip. Barnabas Ministry uses a series of questions to help the leader identify their next steps. The questions focus on both the personal and private life of the leader together with their professional ministry. Coaching session topics include opportunities, barriers, options, and a commitment to a course of action by the leader. As shared above, JCGI has seen many leaders grow in effectiveness both personally and in ministry as they grow and multiply churches. Coaching relationships are an encouraging means of mentoring and equipping others.

Since 2006, JCMN has developed regional coaching groups for pastors to become more effective in their churches. "JCMN Coaching network has grown to have a total of 28 coach pastors spread into 10 regional networks" (Ikubo 2015, 1). These regional networks are located throughout all the regions of Japan.

These networks teach and coach pastors to grasp and implement the core essences of the church. These key principles focus on what local churches should be as primarily the body of Christ: all members participating and empowered by the leadership, everyone dependent on Jesus as the head of the church, their church as part of the kingdom of God, and adaptable structures for ministry (cf. Wong 2010, 107–128).

After developing these regional coaching networks for nearly ten years, JCMN conducted an evaluation of their effectiveness. These networks have had a significant impact in changing the churches to be more like the essence of the church. "Most pastors expressed that their perceptions of church have changed after joining the coaching network. They mostly caught the importance of relationship and the equipping of believers through personal coaching" (Ikubo 2015, 2). Many of the pastors surveyed reported that their church members were doing very well in their new leadership roles.

Their coaching relationships are quite extensive. In some cases, the coaching relationships extend to the fifth generation of coaches. In the JCMN coaching networks, a typical pastor-coach is coaching two to five pastors in coaching networks, some as high as fifteen pastors. Many of the participating pastors see coaching as a key to growth and change and want to coach more pastors (Ikubo 2015, 6). In order to bless more pastors, they feel they should have more training on coaching skills and methodology.

Without a doubt, one-on-one coaching relationships are effective in intentional development of both clergy and lay leadership in local Japanese churches. There is great potential to develop even more leaders for ministry through coaching as more training in these basic skills is exercised by ever-widening groups of churches. Whole groups could benefit by an encouraging coaching culture.

As already seen, coaching can be a powerful tool and an informal means of selecting, training, and developing new leaders.

JAPAN, NATURAL DISASTERS, AND THE CHURCH

Japan is a country that is prone to many natural disasters such as earthquakes, tsunamis, volcanos, and typhoons, which have affected Japanese history and cultural patterns. These have also affected the church and its task of planting the church in Japanese soil, especially with two recent events.

The Great Hanshin Disaster of January 1995, an earthquake that affected the city of Kobe and its environs, was a great shock for the nation and for many pastors and churches. The major lesson from this disaster is that the church was relatively unprepared to even help its own in a large national disaster. Churches and church organizations did not neglect these signs and began preparing for the next natural disaster. On the local level, churches knew their relationships with their community had to change. One example is a pastor in a greatly affected area who knew that, due to damage to his church building, his people could not "come to church" on Sunday for worship services. He encouraged his church members to have church where they were and serve other people around them as they could. The previous pattern of the church was greatly challenged. Lay people were out in the community serving, not merely gathering for worship meetings. This hands-on practical ministry would continue to affect the churches.

The Great Tohoku Triple Disaster on March 11, 2011 was the biggest natural disaster ever to hit Japan. The earthquake was one of the world's largest earthquakes with a magnitude of 9.0. The resultant tsunami was over 125 feet high in some areas. The scale of the disaster affected over eighty-six communities along the northeast coast (see Figure 4). The nuclear accident at the Fukushima power plant became an international concern and would cause many to evacuate their homes, never to return.

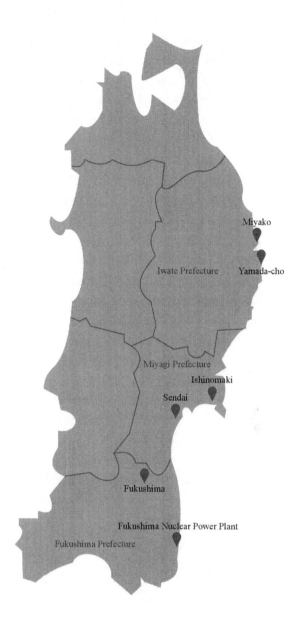

Figure 4. Map of Great East Japan Disaster Area

The amount of damage from this disaster would be recorded as the largest in history ($300 billion). Over eighteen thousand people lost their lives and over 230,000 people lost their homes, creating a diaspora as many were relocated to temporary housing facilities.

At the time of the triple disaster, the Tohoku area was relatively untouched by the gospel. Churches were few and the churches that were meeting were very small, typically ten people or less. There were no missionaries in Iwate Prefecture and only a few in these coastal areas, which share a different culture than areas farther inland. Like the disaster in Kobe sixteen years earlier, the Tohoku disaster created paradigm shifts among Christians and churches.

First was the renewal of the mission of the church and the role of lay people in ministry. The Tohoku disaster "acted as a wakeup call to the churches to seek their missional identities from God" (Wan and Law 2014, 15). Churches were considering their purpose for being and sought God for answers on how best to serve their communities. God continually reminded them that they were there to serve their devastated community. "As a result, many churches started to provide relief aids to the victims and the diaspora" (Wan and Law 2014, 15).

There were many churches and organizations that served in the Tohoku area that "rediscovered their roles and identities as God-sent agents to render services to the suffering communities in Japan and be salt and light to glorify God" (Wan and Law 2014, 16). Wan and Law's research highlights the details of one example of a church working in disaster ministry. The Oasis Chapel in Rifu City, Miyagi Prefecture partnered with one hundred Christian groups by working in several affected locations and ministering in word and deed to thousands of disaster victims. "The overwhelming needs of the communities forced the church to step out of its comfort zone and participate in serving the people in need" (Wan and Law 2014, 79).

Second, previously erected walls were being broken down and removed 1) between Christians and non-Christians, 2) between churches, and 3) between churches and their local communities. The often-repeated story among churches and Christians after the disaster was engagement in ministry across these lines. If God was truly at work, these would be the kind of stories one would expect to hear as God works through his people, his gospel, and his church.

At the time of the disaster most Japanese knew very little about Christianity and likely did not personally know any Christians. After the tsunami, as Christians were mobilized for disaster relief ministry, many people met Christians, sometimes for the first time. For many, this was the first time they had been loved in this manner of grace. Most Christians met physical and emotional needs first, waiting later to share the word of God and Christian truth. This was much appreciated by disaster victims and they were more receptive to the gospel. This developed great bonds of trust and friendship between Japanese and the Christians who came to serve them.

Relationships between local churches were transforming. Before the disaster

> churches in Tohoku were rather isolated. Although there were occasionally fellowships between pastors and joint evangelistic meetings, partnership between churches seldom crossed denominational lines or the partnerships were rather shallow. It was rare for any church to ask for help from churches other than its own denomination. However, right after the disaster, churches immediately realized that they had to join hands together in order to face the challenges posed by the disaster. The needs of the devastated communities and the disaster diaspora were so great that not any single church could do it alone. (Wan and Law 2014, 15)

Churches and their relationship to their communities were also transformed. Many churches were basically unconnected with their communities (Wan and Law 2014, 14). As mentioned above, churches were forced to do ministry in the community because the situation was urgent and desperate. Churches with a new mission perspective continued to be engaged in their communities. At the same time, "Japanese society began to acknowledge the significant contributions of individual Christians and congregations" (Wan and Law 2014, 16).

Often church planting in the disaster area began with relief work and subsequently developing relationships with people within the community. This outward orientation centered on the community and not the church as an organization. This all resulted in churches that were naturally formed from people that were already engaged by Christians in the community. The final stage of church planting was easy: gathering these engaged people for events and church activities.

Large numbers of volunteers came to Tohoku from all over the world and especially from churches all over Japan. Many of these Japanese volunteers returned to their home churches with these paradigm shifts. As these lessons were being learned practically in ministry, not in a classroom, transformation of their perspective and their influence when they returned home was significant. Many Christians and local churches cannot view ministry the same anymore; they are changed. This experience in practical ministry continues to influence the churches that sent these volunteers.

It has been over six years since the Tohoku Triple Disaster. Christian leaders from different faith-based organizations all agree that there has been a spiritual revival in Tohoku (Wan and Law 2014, 1,4). One survey showed that 93 percent of pastors and relief workers felt that there has been change, either some or very much, in the way people see or understand Christianity (Otomo et al. 2016, 67). Some workers have attested that,

"God's Spirit has been active in directly stirring the hearts of the Japanese people" (Yoshimoto et al. 2016, 18).

Christian ministry and church planting has greatly expanded throughout the region affected by the disaster. Reports from a sample of just thirty churches shows an increase of sixty-four baptisms, 178 decisions, and 219 people becoming seekers (Otomo et al. 2016, 55). When compared to the rest of the country, this combined total of nearly five hundred decisions (see Table 5) is an amazing response rate of over 6.5 times what we see in a normal church!

Table 5. Sample Spiritual Response Rate in Tohoku

	Number of Churches	Baptisms	Decisions	Seekers	Total
Churches before the Disaster	10	26	10	34	70
Churches & Ministry Points after the disaster	20	64	178	219	461
Total	30	90	188	253	531

Source: (Otomo et al. 2016, 55)

The Miyagi Mission Network (MMN) reports in Table 6 that before the disaster there were twenty-two churches and after the disaster the number of churches and ministries totals sixty (Otomo et al. 2016, 43). These churches are involved in several types of ministries for evangelism and church planting while addressing needs in the community (ibid., 52–53).

Table 6. Miyagi Prefecture Increase in Churches

Churches before the Disaster	Churches after the disaster	Ministry Points after the disaster	Total
22	19	19	60

Source: (Otomo et al. 2016, 43)

Iwate Prefecture at the time of the disaster had no missionaries; now it has over thirty. Many of these missionaries are from Japan and other Asian countries like China and Singapore. Many villages in Iwate Prefecture like Yamada-cho had no churches, but now it is reported that every city and village has either a church or some ongoing Christian ministry.

The city of Ishinomaki, one of the largest cities of the region with a population of 150,000, experienced massive destruction and about five thousand deaths. The city before the disaster had just seven churches, including one that was about to disband, and most of those churches had ten people in regular attendance. Today there are over thirteen churches meeting in Ishinomaki, and most churches have increased attendance, some averaging over thirty.

Churches partnered to maximize revival in the area that God provided, and so the growing Miyagi Mission Network (MMN) has sixty churches and organizations connected with it (Otomo et al. 2016, 43). "The leaders were committed to meet every month and plan together to strategically serve the diaspora and to plant new churches at different devastated areas" (Wan and Law 2014, 15). The churches are organized into five blocks for cooperation and support (see Otomo et al. 2016, 38–54; Otomo 2016, 99–122). There is also another larger regional network in northeast Japan of the three prefectures of Iwate, Miyagi, and Fukushima connecting with churches for similar purposes.

In April 2016, a series of large earthquakes hit Kumamoto Prefecture on the southern island of Kyushu. Dozens of people died, many were injured, and over 180,000 became homeless. Within a few weeks it was evident that lessons learned in these earlier disasters were being applied in this new disaster: (1) All local churches were networked to provide one central Christian relief organization and (2) relief groups and churches from other parts of Japan were connecting with this organization to provide supplies and ministry volunteers. Ministry was on the ground and running within days—many with people experienced in Tohoku and other places—with the purposes of evangelism and church planting. This is a direct result of mobilizing churches for disaster and networking them in their regions through disaster relief organizations like CRASH, DRC Net, and the JEA Disaster Relief Commission.

These changes among Christian believers and local churches that resulted from the disaster are very much welcomed. However, there is a concern that in the fulfillment of disaster relief ministry, which is a valid ministry in its own right, ministry in word and deed will result in ministry in deed only and the task of the church to disciple the nations through new churches will be lost. Trends are occurring even within evangelical circles which cause this writer significant concern. Is the mission of the church being redefined to disregard proclamation of the gospel? Or are churches simply learning how to be more relevant in connecting with their communities by ministries of word and deed?

CONCLUSION

This chapter outlined several ministries, trends, patterns, and networks that have developed to make the gospel relevant in the Japanese context and to promote church health toward growing and multiplying churches. As we look back, we can apply in our time some of the great potential of principles and practices that have been valuable in transforming Japanese society through the multiplication of gospel-centered churches.

With this background, the next few chapters will outline current effective models of church reproduction and characteristics of reproducing church leaders. We now turn our attention to models that are effectively reproducing the church in Japan.

EFFECTIVE MODELS
OF REPRODUCING
CHURCHES IN JAPAN

There have been glimmers of hope in multiplying churches in Japan. We have just looked at examples of growing church movements, social movements in Japan, and trends in church planting that can be a base for multiplying the church. In this chapter we will focus on a few currently effective models for reproducing the church in Japan. Before turning to these models, we will begin with a preliminary discussion on philosophy of church ministry and then review the common model used in Japan to plant churches.

Today there is a growing understanding of the nature of the church worldwide. There is a rediscovery, recovery, and renewal regarding the doctrine of the church. In our rapidly changing world, many desire to see biblical Christianity incarnated in the church and relevant in modern culture. This comes as the church responds and engages many issues in the world such as globalization, urbanization, the diaspora of peoples, and the development of the church in the two-thirds world. As a result, there has been a renewed interest in the nature, essence, and meaning of the church as it is expressed locally. This has caused many people to again search the scriptures, study church history, rethink the church theologically, and experiment practically with new models of the church.

Some new paradigms and perspectives on the church have led many leaders and churches to develop new models as contemporary examples of the local church. Some movements like the emerging church have come with helpfulness as well as some caution. This reformation in the understanding of the church as it has been traditionally understood and practiced often is accompanied by a renewal of church organization and infrastructure. The desire to achieve a healthy, culturally relevant, growing, indigenous, multiplying church has resulted in many shifts in emphasis and application.

Some shifts have placed more emphasis on the church as the people of God rather than the church as an institution. More emphasis has been given to the organism of the church as created by the Spirit than to its organization created by the work of man. Many have moved away from the cathedral or parish model of the church to more organic types of churches, especially in terms of the forms and structures of the church. In many cases, there has been a shift to a simpler and more basic type of church. Many are also rediscovering the missionary nature of the church and the church's mission commitment to its community and the world. A movement of the missional church has gathered interest in both Europe and North America to turn around churches that are focused on institution and themselves. This has resulted in different philosophical models of ministry, types of church structure, and styles of organization. This affects every aspect of the church including its leadership, activities, and physical location.

Since the book of Acts and throughout church history there have been many different types and models of the church. There are several newer models and paradigms that have developed in North America, Latin America, Europe, and Asia which have forced many pastors and lay people worldwide to rediscover the biblical nature of the church. The end result is the development of models that are more mission-focused, such as the seeker-sensitive model or the purpose-driven model. Others have opted for a simpler organic model of the church, such as the cell church and the house church.

From a look at the statistics, the church in Japan is generally not reproducing. The total number of churches has declined five out of the last six years (*Christian Shimbun* 2016, 3). Most local churches are sterile, possibly unhealthy, and have not reproduced. A majority of denominations in Japan have leveled off or are declining (see chapter one). What is certainly necessary is more churches in Japan, both fresh church plants and churches that are reproducing.

PHILOSOPHY OF MINISTRY

Before we get to the actual models, it would be good to review what models are and put them in perspective. Church models are key components of a church's philosophy of ministry. Every church has a statement of faith, history, and a general idea of how they operate or a philosophy of ministry. "A philosophy of ministry is a unique set of ministry purposes, values, styles, strategies and models embraced and used by a person and/or church in doing the work of gospel ministry in a particular cultural context" (Global Church Advancement 2007, 129). A church philosophy of ministry answers many questions. It begins with very broad questions on the theology of the local church:

- Why does THE church exist? (Vision)
- What is THE church to do? (Purposes)

Every church should display the "fundamental" biblical purposes and functions of the church. The church teaches the Word, prays, fellowships together, worships, and witnesses to all for the glory of God (cf. Acts 2:42–47). Then the questions become more specific for this local church and its context.

- What are the core motivations for THIS church ministry? (Values)
- How does THIS church do gospel ministry? (Styles and Strategy)
- What are THIS church's unique ministry plans? (Mission & Model)

The church's mission and strategy can be summed up in these questions:

- WHO are we here to serve?
- WHAT are their greatest felt and real needs?
- HOW are we planning to help meet these needs? (ibid., 129)

Also, each church is unique in its setting and has a unique personality as it works out its philosophy of ministry. In following the biblical requirements of a church, each local church might emphasize them in a variety of ways; they may have a different style of worship or leadership, or they may have a completely different strategy to accomplish God's purposes in that context. Indeed, a philosophy of ministry for a particular church is not unlike a "theological vision" that is "a faithful reinstatement of the gospel with rich implication for life, ministry, and mission in a type of culture at a moment in history" (Keller 2012, 19).

CHURCH MODELS

Another way to understand how the fundamental biblical purposes and functions are lived out in the church is in the concept of church models. A church model "is a form or expression of the local church that is culturally defined by both the church planters and the people they are serving, in light of the biblical parameters of what constitutes a church" (Payne 2009, 311). Church models are based on the biblical requirements and applied theology of the church. A model is dependent on the cultural understanding of both the church planter and those they are trying to reach. A model is merely a form or expression and should not be seen as the final word on what a church is.

Usually church models are seen in broad-based categories on the type of church. For example: parish model church, megachurch, house church, urban neighborhood church, seeker sensitive church, rural regional church, etc. Often in literature and in discussions on models there is much enthusiasm and passion for one church model over another. Sometimes these lead to confusion, posturing, and occasionally anger. There is a need to understand church models in a broader perspective.

CHURCH MODELS IN PERSPECTIVE

1.   First, focus must be on biblical principles, not models. We should always be unified and major on the biblical principles and the non-negotiable essentials of the church. We should then minor on applications, examples, and models. Principles ultimately are central, not the models of the church. When doing ministry, we should not simply copy models but endeavor to copy and apply the principles behind the models.

2.   God loves and honors his church no matter what model. We must rejoice in the variety that God has given to his church, the bride he deeply loves. No matter what type of church, as fellow believers and members of God's church, we should celebrate with them as God is working. In spite of our minor differences, God highly values the unity of his church. We are to love the church no matter what type or size it is. Let us embrace and value all the models of the church.

3.   There is always much to learn from each other. We acknowledge there is much to learn from other models even if it is not necessarily the model one would personally advocate. The hope is that a fresh look at the essential church principles and strengths realized in a particular model will radically affect current practices. Everyone should be careful with assumptions, especially over definitions of what constitutes a local church, leadership roles and qualifications, church activities and requirements, and physical locations of ministry. Cultivating this learning posture will protect us from potential elitist and judgmental attitudes that may lead to disruptiveness. Some are trailblazers in applying biblical principles more consistently. This may necessitate some patience with other believers who are not nearly as far along. For some believers, some of these proposed changes can appear threatening to our current church systems. In faith, we must learn and then embrace those principles and changes that are necessary to bring God glory in his church.

4.   Realize there are no pure models now, and there will always be a newer model. This is healthy and expected. As culture changes and as we understand better what the church is to be, we will develop new approaches and models of the church.

5.   One model does not fit every context. We affirm that not every model or application is appropriate for every situation. Depending on the context, just as in the New Testament, there are many ways to "do church." The church is not like a McDonalds, or a 7-11 convenience store franchise where every church should be exactly the same. The true mark of a local church is that it should engage with its cultural context to transform it. Anyone leading or planting a church will have to do the hard work of developing their own model on the principles others have developed, but each context is unique. Whatever direction is chosen, the best advice is to keep it very simple.

6.   Transitioning models is not easy or sometimes even possible. Many experts believe that it is nearly impossible to transition a more standard church model into a simple cell or house church. Church practitioners in Japan have found with great focus and energy churches can transition to cell churches. However, many of them advocate applying some of the principles to help bring renewal to the standard model. They also insist that a standard church can serve as an effective base in planting more simple cell and house churches. We also must recognize that for various reasons, some leaders may not currently have the freedom to change or transition to another church model.

7.   Future models will certainly look different. Models and applications of the church do change with time. Therefore, we must be open to what God may be doing in the future. Even though they are relatively recent, already there are several sub-models of cell churches and house churches that have developed. The "missional community" model was introduced in Japan over the last few years and implementation will take some time.

THE COMMON CHURCH
PLANTING MODEL IN JAPAN

After Japan opened again for trade in 1859, Protestant missionaries began entering Japan. At first their movements were restricted to the major cities of Hakodate, Tokyo, Yokohama, Kobe, Nagasaki, and a few other places. Their religious activities were also restricted as it was illegal to convert people to the Christian religion. Most missionaries began educational work in various subjects and presented Christianity as part of the increased interest in Western thought and learning. Alongside churches, mission schools were developed to influence the Japanese. When the religious restrictions were lifted in 1873, this education-based approach was continued with the intent of winning students to Christ.

Yamamori has classified this dominant church planting model as "the school approach" by citing Mutsuro Sugii's study on conversion patterns during this early period. "The school approach then may be characterized by the intellectual and individualistic response to the Christian faith" (Yamamori 1974, 58). Churches during that period primarily consisted of young students, individuals, often many women (Yamamori 1974, 127). This "school approach" model had several features. "Christianity was understood as a learning. The convert joined the church after a long period of study" (Yamamori 1974, 127). It required a clergyman to take the role of teacher, and a building with land needed to be secured.

In the post-war period, mission agencies and denominations have been primarily using this model to plant the church. This "common model" to plant churches in pioneering areas is viewed as a one-size-fits-all model. Features of the common or traditional model for church planting in Japan resemble the school approach. The church is often clergy-centered, dependent on a building or meeting place, and focused on the Sunday worship service. Its evangelistic pattern, like the school model, uses a direct front-door attraction model for evangelistic meetings in the church. These churches are typically single-celled without small groups, connected with the community predominantly through concern for spiritual matters or education in Christianity, and primarily defined by their activities and programs.

Forty-five years ago, Neil Braun described the typical method of planting churches in Japan as pioneer evangelism: "The most common method of starting a new church in Japan . . . is for a Church or Mission to send one or two professional clergymen to the locality and subsidize their activity. In areas where no churches exist, or where the existent churches are not missionary, this is doubtless one method which may be followed" (1971, 31). Because there are still hundreds of places needing their first church, the day of missionaries and Japanese pioneering churches is not over. However, Braun questions the effectiveness of the common method when considering the great task of evangelism needed in Japan. "But as a method it is clumsy, slow, and inordinately expensive. Moreover, it seldom involves the laity, being almost wholly clergy-centered. This way of multiplying churches can never win Japan" (ibid.). The past forty-five years has proven this assertion that "existing churches in Japan seldom start new churches (ibid., 30).

A recent field study of reproducing Japanese churches concluded,

> Some churches, without the cooperation of other churches, in a period of ten years could not reproduce their own church. Church planting workers find the task very difficult, expending 6–12 years or more, to get a church to a degree of stability in active numbers, ministry, organization and finances. This difficulty is compounded in a traditional church planting model by the considerable financial outlay to hire a full-time seminary-trained pastor and acquire land and a building. At present, there are few churches actually reproducing and many of those only have enough resources to start one church and therefore do not multiply. (Mehn 2010, 14)

Over the last three decades with the introduction to Japan of different church models and church planting approaches, some mission agencies and denominations have been willing to investigate and even experiment with new church planting models. Nonetheless, the "common model" of church planting continues in some circles to be understood as *the* method for church planting and is often employed by many Japanese denominations and mission agencies. What is needed in models of church planting are elements often missing from the "common model." These are:

- Increased engagement with the community
- A leadership pattern which includes lay leadership and sometimes clergy
- Small groups
- Along with church activities (attraction), outreach in multiple locations (scattering evangelism)
- Evangelism which reaches whole families
- Lay people mobilized for evangelism and leadership
- Reproducing disciples, leaders, and churches

EFFECTIVE MODELS FOR CHURCH REPRODUCTION

Presented here are six effective models for reproducing the church in Japan. These were selected by field research, interviews, personal observation, and ministry reflection with many missionaries and pastors. While other church growth criteria are certainly important (effective evangelism, discipling, leadership development, etc.), the crucial criteria is that they are models that reproduce churches and they demonstrate effective principles for working in the Japanese context. The church examples are predominately led by Japanese leaders and only two examples are currently led by a missionary.

The models are shared here with some qualifications. They are not neat packages. They are not exclusive models and sometimes overlap. In some cases, I have chosen my own terminology.

The attempt is to be as comprehensive as possible but there might be other effective models that are not included here. The examples given are for illustration and should not be considered the only example or even the finest example. These six models are not presented in any specific order but rather for ease of presentation.

This chapter will summarize six models from field case studies taken from church planting training currently offered in Japan. Along with examples of these models, we hope to highlight the strengths of each model as well as ministry principles applied.

1. Target Penetration Missional Model
2. Network Church Planting
3. Simple Church Networks
4. Cell Church Reproduction
5. Multisite Churches
6. Sending Churches

TARGET PENETRATION MISSIONAL MODEL

This model targets a specific people, begins community engagement, and develops relationship with that target group, leading to small groups and eventually public worship. First, a ministry focus group is identified and studied intensively. The ministry team develops a unique philosophy and approach for that context by interacting with the needs of the focus group and strategizing how to penetrate it with the gospel for transformation. Second, the team enters the target group and begins incarnating the gospel and learning of community and personal needs (missional community approach rather than church programming). Team members are engaging the community and building relationships that increase their understanding of the ministry focus group. The target group is evangelized relationally through personal witness, and as more relationships develop, there are more opportunities for evangelism (see Figure 5). Then they develop relational small groups and build leaders. This continues with team building from the harvest and building missional ministries. They do not establish public worship until they have developed relationships with a significant number of people. When there is a sufficient number of people involved (usually at least 40–70) weekly public worship is "launched." Since the goal is to not plant one church but to launch a movement of multiplying churches, they aim for a strong, growing "first" church for reproduction.

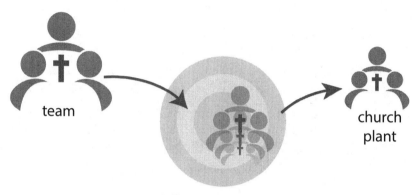

Figure 5. Target Penetration Model

Ministry Examples:

1.   Grace City Church Tokyo (Pastor Makoto Fukuda) moved to their target community in 2009 and invested eighteen months to develop relationships with their target group of young urban professionals and artists in an unchurched region near Tokyo Station. During this time, they met with contacts for one-on-one Bible studies and small community groups, often in coffee shops and restaurants. The team had cultivated about fifty personal relationship contacts before inaugurating public worship. They recruited, trained, and coached some leaders for their community groups. After five years, they have two hundred in two weekly worship services and fourteen community groups. Their daughter church, Grace Harbor Church (Pastor Seima Aoyagi), targeted Toyosu island in Tokyo Bay beginning ministry in 2011. In 2014 this church began monthly worship services that after one year

became weekly. At the time of this writing they are making plans for their own daughter church. These churches are part of the Grace Church Planting Network that has four churches engaged.

2. Jesus LifeHouse (Pastor Rod Plummer) started in 2002 in Tokyo with a team of ten Australians and one Japanese targeting "non-Christian" young people (17–35 year-olds) such as university students and young professionals. Their church is an international church with a bilingual approach. Through personal evangelism they developed many contacts with youth. The church also has many outreach events. They have small groups (called life groups) for discipleship and a system of developing leadership. These mainly meet at convenient times in public locations like coffee shops (Nethercott 2007, 12). By sending out their own trained workers, they have planted thirteen churches in major cities in Japan and several overseas locations (mainly in Asia and Hawaii). The Tokyo cluster of seven locations has about two thousand attending.

Ministry Principles and Evaluation

- The team enters and lives among the ministry focus group they are reaching.
- They incarnationally touch personal, communal, and spiritual needs in the community.
- While interacting with the ministry focus group, they contextualize the gospel through grassroots efforts.
- Relational evangelism is primary and evangelistic events are normally used only after relationships have developed.
- One-on-one and small group learning and growing is emphasized.
- Patience is required to allow the personal relationships to develop until establishing more formal ministries and worship.
- Reproduction is part of the church DNA as everything is reproduced: disciples, leaders, ministries, and churches.

- To develop this team, enter a community, and produce a church demands a lot of upfront resources in manpower and money. However, developing a "beachhead church" has great potential for a church multiplication movement. This end vision must not be lost in the process.
- One key issue is developing a unified team under a point man leader. Assessment, coaching, and support of leaders are crucial.
- This model may be very difficult or nearly impossible to use to plant a church in some rural areas with lower or declining populations.

NETWORK CHURCH PLANTING

Three or more churches partner together in a network to each plant a daughter church within three years. Usually the planted daughter church is a simple church (cell group) and led by a lay person. The purpose of the network is for mutual learning, encouragement, and church multiplication vision, making it easier for each church to plant one daughter church in the three-year time frame. This is a proven system for established churches to reproduce. Asian Access Japan's JCGI Networks provides the training system and participants manual along with a coordinator and an advisor to this regional network that meets monthly. Each church plants their own daughter in a parent church network (see Figure 6 on the next page). Network members focus only on their own church plant and, besides encouragement and prayer, do not have direct connection with the other daughter churches. The leaders of these regional or local networks are encouraged and supported by coaching relationships (called Barnabas ministries).

The first network was started by JCGI in 1996 and has expanded to many regions such as Hokkaido, Kanto, Kansai, Kyushu, and Okinawa. JCGI Networks welcomes churches to consider forming a network in their area for church multiplication.

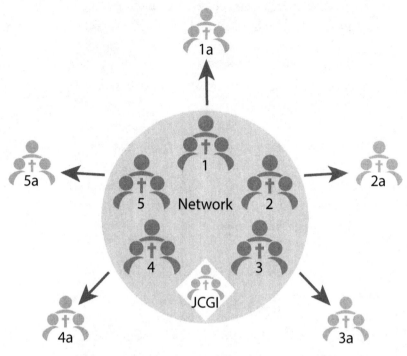

Figure 6. Network Church Planting

Currently, there are nearly thirty of these networks throughout all regions of Japan. From the beginning, nearly fifty churches have been planted with a potential for another fifty.[6] The fact that Japanese networks often include churches from different associations is quite incredible compared to other countries where networks usually consist of churches within the same denomination. The cross-fertilization of ideas is far more possible. The network is usually formally discontinued after the three-year period, but often, strong relationships remain to continue similar church multiplication vision in their region.

---

6.   For further explanation of network functions in detail, see Kawasaki 2002.

Ministry Example:

1. The Yamagata Project started in 1996 with five churches that each established five new churches within the three-year cycle. These same five mother churches then began in 1999 with a second cycle along with their new daughter churches to plant granddaughter churches in the Yamagata Project No 2.

2. The Sendai Church Multiplication Network started in 2004 with six churches. Three churches were birthed by the completion of the network in 2006. Through this process, several churches underwent a paradigm shift and renewed their vision for church multiplication and lay ministry. Shortly after that in the same region, the Tohoku Miyagi Network was formed in 2007 with four churches, and the church multiplication vision was enlarged. This network met until 2010, one year before the triple disaster in the region. After the disaster in 2011, these same churches, earlier networked for church planting, were instrumental in forming the Miyagi Mission Network[7] that has expanded evangelism, church multiplication, and disaster relief among an even larger number of churches throughout the area.

Ministry Principles and Evaluation:

- The network makes it easier for each church to plant one daughter church.
- Simple churches with lay leadership are easier to birth.
- This is a proven model over decades and in various settings.
- As a daughter church model, there are some practical limitations on distance and time between the daughter and mother church.
- The intention is to involve many lay people from the beginning of the network. Sometimes this is not realized as clergy can often meet more easily.

---

7. See also pages 87–88.

SIMPLE CHURCH NETWORKS

A "house church" is a simple church usually led by lay people that meets in homes, rental locations, or public places like coffee shops, restaurants, or karaoke boxes. Often, each church is loosely connected to other simple churches for networking. Sometimes there will be joint leadership training for several simple churches or even networks (see Figure 7).

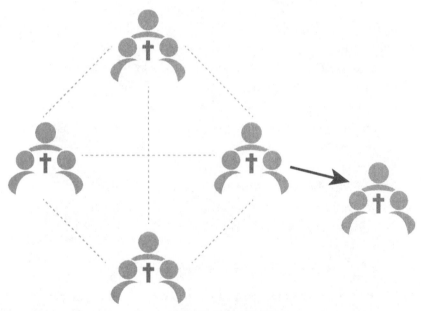

Figure 7. Simple Church Networks

There are several multiplying networks of dozens of lay led "house" churches mainly in the Tokyo and Osaka areas (Fujino 2007, 2–3). Since the triple disaster in Tohoku other networks have formed there. One network has discipleship reproduction to the seventh generation where thirty to forty people meet in two house groups. These simple churches can easily hive off or birth new churches (see Fujino 2009; Cozens 2010).

Ministry Examples:

1. Be One Network (Chad Huddleston) started their ministry in 2000 in Osaka based on the command of Jesus in John 17:21 to "be one." Through discipleship ministries, Life Transformation Groups and Ten-Nai-Gai training several house churches were started. Currently there are six house churches meeting in Osaka, Kyoto, and Shiga Prefectures using homes and three of the groups meet on different days using the same rental space. They have also used beauty parlors, medical clinics, restaurants, and coffee shops for meetings. A joint worship celebration is often monthly and the leaders also meet regularly for joint training.

In 2011, after the triple disaster, this simple church network became very active in relief work in Tokoku. The network was involved in disaster relief and clean up, along with evangelism and discipleship ministry establishing another ministry base. Worship services began in a home in the Watanoha community that has grown to about forty people who meet weekly in their outreach sports center. They often break into three house church groups. One group meets at the Nozomi Project, which is a business established to help disaster victims earn a living making jewelry. Church leaders have regular training and together they are targeting the next generation.

2. Kanto House Church Network was launched in 2006 originally targeting young people ages 19–30 but has widened to minister to others. Though originally led by missionaries, it is now led by Japanese leaders. The network has at least eight churches in over six areas meeting throughout the Kanto area such as Ochanomizu, Matsudo, Tokorozawa, Shinagawa, Kanagawa, and Tokyo. The churches of the network use homes, dance studios, karaoke boxes, medical clinic offices, and other business offices for their worship meetings. The network has regular training for the leaders usually monthly. They are also training and coaching other house church leaders outside their network.

Ministry Principles and Evaluation:

- This newer-style model of the church seems more advantageous to church planting reproduction as it emphasizes simpler structure, small groups, and mobilizes lay leadership for ministry.
- These simple churches foster close relationships and share church leadership through teamwork.
- Hardly any organizational structures are needed to start these simple churches.
- Simple churches are born rapidly but unfortunately also often disappear rapidly. To support all the churches and keep them from vanishing, networks are doing more inter "church" meetings such as monthly celebration gatherings.
- Groups meeting in homes, especially for religious purposes, are viewed by many Japanese as impermanent, suspicious, and sometimes cult-like, in contrast to meeting in more public locations like coffee shops and offices.

CELL CHURCH REPRODUCTION

Cell churches have two main fellowship functions 1) a large group "celebration" worship meeting and 2) many "cell" or small groups. These cell groups are not unlike simple churches where the focus of church life occurs (see Figure 8). Cell churches reproduce by continually producing new cells groups through 1) direct birthing, 2) partnering to reproduce, or 3) starting a pioneer cell. Some of these cells can easily become autonomous churches. Many of these churches are connected with the Japan Cell Church Mission Network (JCMN).

Ministry Examples:

1.   Hongodai Christ Church—Yokohama (Pastor Hiroshi Ikeda) is a large church with dozens of cell groups (called pastoral families) organized in geographical zones that multiply and divide,

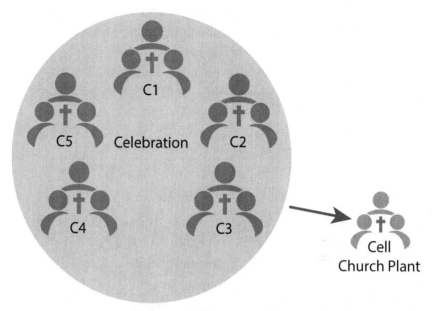

Figure 8. Cell Church Reproduction

forming new cells. A leadership cell supports the leaders of the cell groups called "family shepherds" (Tsukii 2002).

2. Through a cell process, Nerima Grace Chapel—Nerima (Pastor Yoshiya Yokota) has planted the Kiyose Grace Chapel, about thirty minutes away, that has vision for daughter churches. Their 10-40 Vision is to produce at least forty cell churches by 2020 through pioneering, daughtering, and networking cell groups.

3. Teien Christ Church—Sapporo (Pastor Kentaro Matsuda). This church has 100 percent of its members in dozens of cell groups (called *ie no kyōkai* [house church]). Through evangelism and church ministry, they have been able to spontaneously start new cell groups.

Ministry Principles and Evaluation:

- Some have confidence in this model for Japan as providing both close relationships with a large meeting that is a great encouragement to outnumbered Christians.

- Much discipleship and pastoral care occurs in the cell group.
- Recruiting, training, and coaching cell group leaders develops future pastoral leadership.
- Any church reproduction occurring has the resources of the entire congregation, not just a cell or group of cells.
- Reproduction is made very simple by either hiving off a cell or developing a mission cell to plant a cell in a needy location.

MULTISITE CHURCHES

Organizationally, one church meets in multiple locations for worship and other church activities. These worship locations have the same vision, share leadership, and a common budget (see Figure 9). Most Japanese multisites are nearby within a defined city or region. When one of the locations is strong and mature enough, it is easy to spin off and develop the location into a new church.

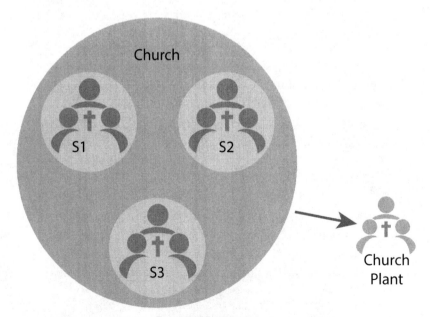

Figure 9. Multisite Churches

Ministry Examples:

1. Oyumino Chapel—Midori Ku Chiba Prefecture (Dan Iverson) has five worship services that meet in three locations near three separate train stations. Each of the four pastors are assigned to one worship location. Because the church is one organization with a common budget, more focus can be placed on evangelism, disciplemaking, and small groups.

2. Dr. Hideo Ohashi presented at the 2009 CPI conference on multisite churches. He highlighted lessons learned from visiting multisite churches in the US and five possible Japanese examples, including Grace Mission Church in the city of Yao in the Kansai area that has fifteen chapels meeting throughout Yao.

Ministry Principles and Evaluation:

- The DNA, values, and vision are the same for each site and can be easily transferred.
- Ministry focus is placed on evangelism and discipleship, not on building an organization.
- Leaders benefit by a team of pastors in community that encourage, assist, and mentor each other.
- Multisite churches free up more roles for leadership, especially for lay people.
- Multisite churches can significantly lower risks in church planting (Stetzer & Im 2016, Kindle location 2509).
- Though the multisite church is a fast-growing area of the American church, this is a rather new phenomenon in Japan. In Japan, most multisite locations have their own "campus pastor" (or the same teaching team) and do not often use videos for messages.

SENDING CHURCHES

These reproducing churches are developing leaders with a church planting vision. In their process of raising up leaders, individuals are encouraged to seek God's vision for their ministry. The church then entrusts them, sends them out, encourages them in their next ministry, and practically helps them with the next steps of church development. They plant daughter churches near the mother church in strategic areas or pioneer through work and school transfers (see Figure 10). Older missionaries referred to this multiplication method as "strawberry evangelism." For more on the leadership of these churches see chapter six.

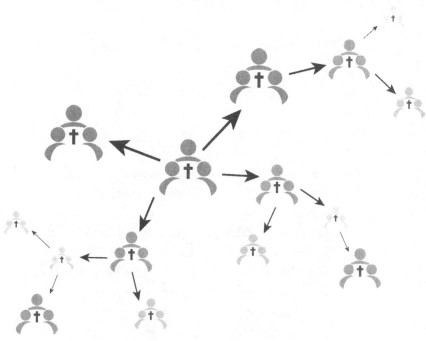

Figure 10. Sending Churches

Ministry Examples:

1. The Keisen Christ Church Network—Yonezawa Yamagata Prefecture (Pastor Jiro Chida) has sent out workers intentionally to other areas as church planters and also through school and work transfers. The church has established over twenty-four churches and several of them have reproduced themselves. The church equips those sent out and supports them through training and coaching.

2. Tokyo Horizon Chapel—Machida City and Setagaya Ward, Tokyo (Pastor Koichi Hirano) has sent out workers to establish fourteen chapels in nearby locations and some as far as Karuizawa and Nagoya. The mother church provides theological training for new workers and supports their church plants through regular visits and coaching.

Ministry Principles and Evaluation:

- Church planting is spontaneously done by equipping people and giving them a vision.
- To raise up leaders, the pastor's main role and priority is developing people.
- Often the new churches started are simple or cell churches.
- These churches and their daughters begin their own networks for encouragement and support.
- They can plant many churches close by, but it demands more focus and resources in pioneering in more distant areas.

A SUMMARY OF PRINCIPLES

What are some overall principles of church planting reproduction in Japan that we can learn from these models? Here is a general summary of the key principles found in these six models.

1. Dream and think big but at the same time work small.
2. Grow a team of leaders, rather than one solo worker or a clergy pastor, that practices continual encouragement, support, and training.
3. Determine a well-defined ministry target by "exegeting" and understanding a ministry focus group and their community. Contextualize the gospel and the church to serve them.
4. Articulate a clear vision and philosophy of ministry; establish systems for evangelism, discipleship, and leadership development; and clarify specific outcomes that set the direction of the ministry.
5. Mobilize lay people for evangelism and ministry leadership.
6. Focus on expanding relational evangelism that is both attractional (coming to worship service, special events, etc.) and missional (going into the community to touch needs and hearts).
7. Utilize small groups for evangelism, fellowship, discipleship, and leadership development.
8. Develop vision and plans for reproduction and multiplication movements that lead to the actual practice of reproduction.
9. Incorporate creative approaches to enhance ministry such as multisite, video in meetings, Skype church, etc.

The reasons these six models have been observed as being effective is that they embody the vital principles of reproduction for evangelism, discipleship, and leadership development that lead to reproducing churches.

EFFECTIVE MODELS AND THE COMMON MODEL

This material was first presented in 2010 to a large group of church planters from dozens of churches and agencies. After the presentation, one experienced leader had a very insightful question. He noticed the list of effective models did not include the typical church planting model in Japan. While this common model was indeed very familiar to the presenters, it was widely seen as generally ineffective in reproducing churches; therefore, it was not listed.

Historically, some Japanese denominations have developed an unintended dependence on foreign missionaries to plant new churches so those new churches can subsequently be led by a Japanese pastor. Many of these church plants were encouraged by these denominations to use this common model. Because there often was no ministry team or intentional leadership development, and no plan for reproduction, these churches had difficulties when the missionary transferred leadership to a Japanese pastor. In some cases, people who were previously attending exited the church and left the Japanese pastor with a much smaller group of people. This whole process was then seen as a partial failure.

Over the years, dozens of common model churches have been started, yet very few have reproduced. This does not mean the common model cannot reproduce churches; it simply means that it does not often occur, raising many questions. People should be challenged to consider the reasons for its ineffectiveness in reproduction and whether it should be promoted. Some see it as continuing ineffective patterns and hindering the advance of churches. This is in stark contrast to other church planters who are capable of "exegeting" communities, developing relationships, evangelizing, building disciples and leaders, and reproducing their churches. As mentioned in chapter three, the Holiness churches made a distinct break from the school approach pattern to church planting because they saw the approach as too intellectual and unable to reach whole families. Instead, they saw far better results with the "Conversion Approach" model for establishing new churches (Yamamori 1974, 120–128). What is needed is a radical departure from a church model that has been anemic and development of models that more faithfully follow biblical principles. This will take risk, but it should bear fruit with more effectiveness.

CONCLUSION

We should rejoice that the church is reproducing in some quarters in Japan. There are a variety of models that are working, indicating that leadership vision for reproduction and the application of ministry principles will result in reproduction. Some of these churches were mentioned as examples. Most likely, the leaders of these churches would not want anyone to completely copy what they do. They realize that their churches, like all churches, are flawed in some way and certainly not perfect. They also know that each community is distinct, but they would be honored if others learned from them and possibly improved their ministries. To fulfill the work of God in Japan, we all have so much to learn.

Having discussed various effective models for reproducing the church in Japan, we now turn to the next chapter and examine leaders of reproducing churches and their leadership characteristics.

LEADERS REPRODUCING CHURCHES

Experts have stressed that the church leader, as well as the leadership community of a church, is one of the most crucial factors in church reproduction. "Many studies have confirmed the fact that the most important institutional variable for the growth and expansion of the local church is leadership" (Wagner 1990, 20). Leadership has already been shown to be a key factor in the planting of churches, and leadership is confirmed as a key factor in church reproduction and multiplication.

Japan, despite its obvious leadership needs, has many capable and highly educated church leaders. Reflecting on the church situation in Japan, however, it seems unfortunate that most of these leaders have not contributed to the reproduction of the church (Moore 2009, 174). One Japanese research group assesses the lack of gospel fruit in Japan as attributable to the lack of maturity of pastors and other church leaders (Research F Group 2014, 16–20).

If the church in Japan is to reverse the declining status quo and grow through reproduction, the leadership factor, along with other essential factors, must be addressed. More leaders like those of churches that are effectively reproducing and multiplying need to be identified and developed. Understanding the unique qualities and behaviors of these church-reproducing leaders can make a major contribution in changing the entire leadership landscape in the church in Japan.

This chapter describes results from research into leadership characteristics of reproducing churches in Japan (Mehn 2010).

This field research was conducted on over sixty churches that had reproduced at least three churches over a twenty-year period. These churches were surveyed with a questionnaire to determine basic information. Of the thirteen churches that completed the questionnaire, six churches—which planted a total of sixty-two churches—were selected for in-depth semi-structured interviews. Six primary and eight secondary leaders were interviewed about personality, giftedness, leadership development, theological perspective, role, style, priorities, behavior, and practice of church reproduction. These six reproducing churches are situated in different areas of Japan, are different sizes, are from different denominations and church traditions, and have diverse styles of ministry, including traditional, cell, and house church models.

Reproducing churches, especially in a difficult country like Japan, demands a special kind of leader. Data analysis of field research revealed six distinctive preliminary characteristics for these leaders of reproducing churches, which were confirmed by the pastors interviewed and another house church leader. These six characteristics seem interrelated and should not be considered independently.

1. God-Given Ministry Vision
2. Risk-Taking Faith
3. View of the Church as a Dynamic Sending Community
4. Development of Lay People for Ministry
5. Relational Leadership through Encouragement
6. Aggressive Implementation through Practical Ministry

GOD-GIVEN MINISTRY VISION

International leadership studies surveying leadership in dozens of countries have concluded that one key characteristic of a "transformational leader" includes developing a future vision and communicating that vision to followers. This is true for global business leaders and for Japanese leaders in particular (House et al. 2004).

Leadership studies are revealing that vision is a vital component of any effective leadership in the church (Barna 1997; Okawa 2002, 44–46). Vision studies on Japanese church leaders show that those with a large vision are very effective in church planting and reproduction (KDK 1986; Solheim 1986; JEA 1988; Satake 1994; Guthrie 1995; Kawasaki 2002).

Leaders are expected to be called by God and have a vision and a direction for ministry. One reproducing pastor said, "A local church is built according to the plan of God. If you do not know God's plan, you do not know where the church should go. An important role of a leader is to learn the direction [of the church] from God and clearly show it [to the people]." For this research, it was estimated that vision would be an important factor in the leadership of these Japanese church-reproducing leaders. How and where their ministry vision came from was surprising.

Listening to God

These leaders displayed spiritual sensitivity; they had an openness to God and his Spirit. If vision is best caught rather than taught, who better to listen to than God? One pastor affirmed, "It is more than 'we have a plan'; it is that 'we have God's plan.' Pray and keep quiet before God. Listen to God." This quality of spiritual sensitivity was also confirmed in interviews of other secondary leaders who knew these pastors.

The receiving of vision from God grew out of these leaders' prayer lives. Until God revealed his vision, one pastor prayed weekly and another prayed for several months. Another pastor spent two hours at a seminar listening to God about the direction for his life. He felt that traditional [leadership] style was "restricted" in listening to God for direction, saying:

> Although we were working very hard, we
> neglected the practice of listening to God to

receive his direction. . . . It is important to have a firm relationship with God and listen to Him about what He wants in his ministry. Whether he fasts or prays all night is a free choice dependent on the culture of that church. But I think the first step is to receive the vision from God in living relationship with Him.

God's Vision from Scripture

As expected, leaders have many influences in their life, but when it came to vision for these leaders none was greater than Scripture. "As for the influence on church multiplication, I don't think that anyone taught me about this method. I feel that this is something God showed me," said a pastor of his impressions from the book of Acts. In only a short time, his church of only forty people had remarkably grown into five churches.

These leaders would not just listen to God in prayer in a subjective or intuitive approach but would also reflect on God and his purposes revealed in Scripture. One pastor, when asked whether the vision was from the heart or from faith, replied, "No, it was from the Bible. Vision was based on biblical principles." When these leaders discuss the topic of the church, they do not reach for their textbooks, quote their denominational line, or some other pastor. They come at it from their study of the scriptures. "Since our vision must be God's vision, we must gain it from the Scriptures" (Malphurs 1999, 9). God would speak to these leaders through Scripture and the extent of the vision was not just for their church, nor just for Japan, but for a global mission vision.

Vision for Church Reproduction

"Essentially [the] church . . . is on a mission in planting other churches" declared one pastor. For several leaders, reproducing their church was not their original plan, but rather to evangelize or build a big church. One pastor said, "There was no thought of building a reproducing church." For many of these leaders, they later embraced a vision for church reproduction as described in Scripture where the church is a dynamic sending organism.

Still, all of these leaders realize that God's ultimate vision is not just church planting and reproduction, but a bigger end— God's glory, his will, and his Kingdom— and church reproduction is a means to this end. One reproducing pastor affirmed that the vision must outlive the life of the leader and be transferred to new generations of leaders, continuing until the return of Christ.

Obedience to the Vision

To these leaders, just receiving and understanding God's vision is considered insufficient. Like Paul in Acts 26: 19, "I was not disobedient to the vision from heaven." For these leaders, to receive a vision is consequently to obey the vision. The Great Commission as church reproduction is God's will, and they are to follow God's will and obey him zealously. A pastor conveyed well-rounded advice, "Listen to God through worship, prayer, and fasting. He will lead you with guidance. Then obey him without question and overcome anything in the way of obedience."

In general, secular studies affirm that vision comes from the leader, his intuition, creativity, and personality. For Christian leaders, the vision comes from God and is articulated by the leader for God's people through his gifts. These church-reproducing leaders—through their personal ministry calling, their habits of listening to God, and reflecting on scripture—received God's vision for their ministry. Their received visions were to be subsequently obeyed until ultimately fulfilled. This broad topic of God's vision is intimately related to the topic of faith.

RISK-TAKING FAITH

"A local church is built according to the plan of God. If you don't know God's plan, you don't know where the church should go. And what is most important is faith. So what the top leader should do is to receive the vision that God reveals, believe it, and confess it," affirmed one reproducing pastor.

Several of these reproducing leaders became models of vision and courageous, risk-taking faith. For one pastor, "Vision and faith are very important. Even in the difficult times, God will provide." Church planting demands a lot of faith; church reproduction even more so. Another declared, "Faith has to be first" because man cannot accomplish church planting. One pastor summarized, "I cannot do anything; faith does it."

Reproducing leaders exercise faith that overcomes obstacles and even their own weaknesses. Their faith battles discouragement and potential failure. It leads in risky directions. Vision for God's church requires great faith. This faith is not inaction, but it springs leaders into action, according to one church leader.

Assuming Ministry Risk

Most people seem to have an aversion to risks. However, Japanese are even more reluctant because of their shame-based culture and group conformity. Risk means uncertainty, and Japan has been categorized as having a culture that greatly avoids uncertainty (Hofstede 1984, 123). Japanese "feel threatened by uncertain or unknown situations" (Hofstede 1997, 113).

Church planting is fraught with ambiguity and risk, church reproduction even more so, especially in a culture so traditionally resistant to the gospel. A reproducing leader, in the same way as an entrepreneur, must be skilled in "overcoming the traditional risk adverse culture" (Helms 2003, 24). It is expected that courageous faith and uncommon tolerance for risk would result in more effectiveness. These reproducing leaders assume ministry risk on the basis of faith in God and his promises. "God's will is a higher priority than our plans. The basic approach becomes accepting any risk for the sake of [God's will]," said one reproducing pastor.

In one-on-one interviews, leaders were asked about how they take unique risks in faith. One pastor shared about giving up key leaders, money, and gifted people to reproduce churches. He said that leaders must always risk for a larger principle, and always have a risk-taking attitude and posture. Another pastor quit his previous job just because God asked him, and then much later became a pastor. One church leader described his pastor as a "risk-taking pastor in a good sense."

These reproducing leaders move away from security and predictability toward the adventure of following God. "It is God's will; we will assume the risk," affirmed one pastor. Like them, are we willing to risk our reputations, our positions, the approval of others, time, money, and energy for the vision God has given us?

Overcoming Reproducing Obstacles

One of the interview questions asked what hindrances and obstacles they confronted in church reproduction, and how they overcame them. Expectations were: hearing about developing contacts, discipling believers, growing leaders, and securing a meeting place. Many church planters share their "if only" stories—if only they had ten believers, a building, more money, or more leaders in their church—but the leaders interviewed considered this type of thinking decidedly negative and normally would not participate in these discussions. These reproducing leaders use faith to simply overcome these obstacles. They did not want to dwell on potential obstacles but did chat briefly about the issues of buildings and property, funding, and personnel. Many commented that hindrances are normal and simply expected to be met. The issue was not *if* one would confront obstacles, but rather *when*.

One reproducing pastor impressed his church by not accepting the common response, "That's impossible." Instead, he challenged others to think beyond the impossible. Many leaders find solutions to hindrances and obstacles by being creative and flexible, exploring solutions, using wisdom, and being joyful when hindrances are overcome. One church leader stated that his pastor "*kitai shite kureru*" (expects things to happen).

Resisting Personal Discouragement

The reality of discouragement in ministry is very common for church leaders in Japan. Often ministry accomplishments don't meet our expectations. Burnout is also common. These reproducing leaders were asked, "How do you keep from being discouraged, as well as gain self-confidence and grow in faith?" The predominant answer for discouragement was their personal walk with God, their devotional life, and prayer. One reproducing pastor outlined how a leader's personal walk with God grows faith and overcomes uncertainty, saying:

> Our spirituality is related to our *kanren* (connection) with Jesus. We are to develop a trusting and loving *kankei* (relationship) with Jesus. We develop power while we worship. This gives us freedom, a lifeline, and *ikioi* (vigor). When the power comes [from God], as a result, we relax. When we become relaxed before God, then God uses us. This is where quiet inner confidence comes from.

Challenging Potential Failure

Church ministry and reproduction are minefields of potential failure, especially in a shame-based culture like Japan. These reproducing church leaders share a different perspective and procedure when facing potential failure, as explained by one pastor:

> Just do it [church reproduction]. You may succeed, or you may not. It does not matter. But if you do not do it, you do not even fail. If you do it and fail, it is a great resource. There is no greater resource than failure . . . As we fail over and over again, we reflect. There is no guarantee that church planting will succeed . . . We make a lot of mistakes while we plant churches.

Faith encompasses active obedience, not fear. "Like in the book of Acts, we looked for God's 'go signs' of opportunity in ministry," said one pastor. Confident faith allows another pastor to say, "God will always lead his church to be the body of Christ." Because of faith, these leaders are able to attempt great ministries with courage and even turn potential failure into a positive outcome.

Summary

These courageous leaders take God's promises seriously and, in faith, depend on God to supply all that is needed to be obedient to the Great Commission. This is the kind of faith we as leaders are encouraged to imitate (Heb 13:7).

By assuming ministry risk, overcoming obstacles, resisting personal discouragement, and challenging potential failure, these reproducing church leaders exercise their faith. Hebrews chapter eleven constantly repeats the phrase, "in faith." Without God's power through faith, leaders cannot build the church—because God alone builds his church. Molded by the vision received from God and an inner-faith confidence in God, these leaders apply their unique view of the church (*kyōkaikan*) to reproduce churches.

VIEW OF THE CHURCH AS A DYNAMIC SENDING COMMUNITY

The most unexpected aspect of this research was every leader remarked on their "view of the church" (*kyōkaikan*). Their comments were more than reciting textbook ecclesiology, since they practically envision the church as a spiritual, organic, dynamic sending community spontaneously growing and reproducing. In some sense, their rich and deep view in defining the church goes beyond reproduction. In their biblical understanding of the church, the people of God, unbound by cultural Christianity, are missionally sending others out in transformational ministry.

A Relational Community

For these leaders, a church is a kaleidoscope of people in association, the body of Christ (1 Cor 12:27–28). They picture the church as primarily people and not an organization or club. Several leaders used the biblical concept of community as their most prominent visualization of the church. These communities form and increase naturally. One pastor affirmed, "When the gospel is preached it forms a community of Christ. It is essential that many of these communities increase wherever it is necessary." The church is to accomplish all that is necessary to be a healthy community and body of Christ (Ott & Wilson 2011, 15). This church view means the community is simply "to be," not necessarily to complete a task, like church reproduction. Rather church reproduction is seen as a natural function of this dynamic community growing and reproducing.

A Dynamic Living Organism

These reproducing leaders view the church as a living organism: it is healthy, growing, increasing, multiplying, and expanding. These leaders comprehend the church as a live dynamic organism. One pastor pictured the church as a flowing, growing river from the book of Ezekiel where a river emanated from the Temple (Ezek 47). Like this image, the church flows, moves, and, as this pastor said, "The church cannot stop."

These dynamic understandings of a spontaneous church resist preservation of a static ministry of stability or security. This has implications for planning and making strategy. One pastor summarized, "We do not plan anything. So for instance, we do not plan that we need to start a church there or here. . . . We just go with [the] flow. When God is doing some work in that area we just go with it."

Growing organisms are sometimes hard to define due to their fluid nature. Christian Schwarz has written that the church as an organism should not be solely defined by its structure. While organization may help grow the church today, it may hinder the growth tomorrow (Schwarz 1996, 30–31).

A Reproducing Church

Having a healthy and growing church does not only mean becoming larger. Several of these pastors conveyed they were first interested in growing a large church. Then they had a transformative experience where they realized they also must reproduce many churches. These leaders insist reproduction is central to the scriptures and God's primary strategy for the local church to complete the Great Commission (Matt 28:18–20). Several leaders deliberately discontinued their desire to grow a big church so they could have a bigger impact through church reproduction.

These reproducing church leaders believe the church to be reproducing in its essence, which is not a matter of organization or program. In their view, churches are not manufactured but multiplied as a natural result of a dynamic organism expanding and reproducing. This is naturally in the DNA of the church with the hope that every church will reproduce. For these leaders, the time for reproduction is now, as a pastor asserted, "We were not waiting until we became large."

Stuart Murray affirms reproduction is essential to defining the essence of the church (Murray 2001, 62–63). For these leaders, reproduction is normal and natural. When asked why their churches are exceptions in church reproduction, the leaders said they doubted they were exceptions, they have done only a minimum, or they are simply ordinary. Church reproduction according to one pastor is "natural if you are a church. . . . This is something the church does. Reproducing churches are nothing special. . . . It is normal; it is standard and average." Not to reproduce would be unnatural and abnormal.

A Sending Mission

For these leaders the church is imagined as a sending mission that grows from the church's deep evangelistic purpose and motivation as well as the practical need for evangelism in Japan. This missional spirit moves the church away from being protective and defensive. One reproducing pastor quoted earlier described their mission philosophy, "We are not defensive. 'Offensive' does not sound good, but we are not becoming busy inside the church but trying to do things outside. . . . if we go out, there are plenty of places for ministry." Being missional means to aggressively reach out and look beyond themselves. The directional orientation of the church is outward. The biblical local church, by its very nature, "is seen as essentially missionary" (Bosch 1991, 372).

One pastor shared about a transformation in his church where instead of inviting people to worship in a building, "we started having the image of going. In order to influence this community, we did not [continue] the 'please come' [approach]." Rather than gathering and attracting, the missional church means scattering and sending.

The church as a missional group becomes a development center to send its own to evangelize and reproduce the church. One pastor explains, "We expand churches to reach those who do not know Christ, which is why people are sent." This mission of sending is accomplished by measuring those who have the desire and burden to plant new churches. Then, according to another pastor, "people are trained and sent out." To these leaders the church continues in its basic mission of evangelism, training disciples, raising people up to then send out to reproduce the church. The church is like a relational community, says another pastor; the church is "always going out, sending out people, expanding [ministry]."

Summary

These leaders envision the church as a dynamic relational community growing naturally and reproducing itself by sending community members into like-minded mission. These churches and their leaders continually refresh and reform themselves by reflecting on the biblical principles for the church. These reproducing leaders challenge the common understanding of a local church. They are not satisfied until their vision of the church is seen in reality. The practical leadership of these leaders of reproducing churches "grows out" of their applied theology of the church.

This unique view of the church (*kyōkaikan*) means these leaders must also have a different "view of the pastor" (*bokushikan*). These leaders do not see the pastorate as a job to perform religious ceremonies for a stable group of people. One church-reproducing pastor shared his major role was to win, disciple, and send others into ministry. For these church leaders, their theological view of the church and their role as a sending agency means mobilizing lay people who have gifts for church reproduction.

DEVELOPMENT OF LAY PEOPLE FOR MINISTRY

When asked about how Japanese reproducing church leaders enable people to catch shared vision for church reproduction, all six primary leaders confirmed the importance of developing and mobilizing lay people. These leaders develop lay people by sharing ownership of the vision for church reproduction, preparing people for practical ministry, and entrusting responsibility to them.

Mobilize Lay People

To fulfill the Great Commission by planting churches in Japan, there will not realistically be enough professional pastors and missionaries. Practically speaking, Japanese lay leaders must be developed and mobilized to do the ministry (Pease 1989, 113).

Hesselgrave believes the church in Japan does not mobilize lay people because of the lack of understanding of the scriptures (Fukuda 2002, 174). These reproducing pastors defend their leadership practices using Scripture, as they understand the laity with the restored original meaning—"the people of God" (1 Pet 2:9–10) called to ministry (Gibbs 2005, 132–33). Ohashi affirms the clergy-laity "gap" remains a systemic problem in training church leaders and traditional church structure where some are viewed as elite and others more common (Ohashi 2007, 142–43). According to one pastor, this clergy-laity gap does not have to exist as "ordinarily the essential principle is we are mutually equal on the same basis as the Lord's people under God's authority. Equally, the pastor and the believers are the Lord's people. . . . The pastor is not the only leader in the church; it also extends to the lay people." These leaders mobilize lay people that affect the relationships, authority, and structure of the church.

Share Ownership of the Vision

These leaders declared many times the value of nurturing joint ownership of vision for reproducing churches. Workers get involved not based on the leader's goals but, according to one pastor, the leader is to "share together with them about the vision and the purpose given from God." In a sense, the leader's role is both a vision-catcher and a vision-caster. One pastor shared, "An important role of a leader is to learn the direction of the church from God and clearly show it to the people." In order to grow vision with believers, one leader mentioned his church had a vision night, and they often discuss in small groups how to fulfill God's plan and purposes.

The purpose of vision sharing is to nurture joint ownership for God's vision. One reproducing pastor mentioned how sharing his long-range church planting dream with the church has nurtured a growing ownership by the people and leaders. Several pastors discussed the importance of the leadership team members sharing ownership for the pastor's church planting passion and being actively involved. This casting and catching of vision must permeate various generations. One pastor mentioned in his interview how the ministry vision began with a missionary, then was passed to his pastor, and now this leader is passing on the vision to young people in his church. "The pastor's influence is to cast the vision and spread it," he said.

Prepare People for Ministry

Leaders mobilize people for ministry by helping lay people discover God's intended service for them, preparing them, and deploying them. As people want to be used by God, every believer should be mobilized, whether or not they end up planting churches. One pastor described the overall process of preparing people: "Evaluate those who have received the burden to plant churches from God. Evaluate their desire if it truly comes from the Lord. Then have the people around them also think about [their suitability]. . . . Then if it is okay, we will send them out."

These leaders accept lay people as full leaders and deploy them to establish and develop churches. Their qualifications for leadership selection are very simple; they are persons who have a calling from God, have spiritual character, and are gifted by the Holy Spirit. Such persons are then affirmed by the church for ministry. They are encouraged to seek God's vision, understand their gifts and ministry opportunities, and are encouraged to venture out in service. These lay leaders are respected as part of the leadership team as equals under the sovereign control of the Chief Shepherd.

Preparation begins with a worker's ministry call. Workers are called to evangelism as God prepares people to cooperate in fulfilling his plan. This is often based on their personal desire to do something for God. As each leader has been given gifts for ministry and work, leaders need to use their gifts in ministry in order to make the greatest impact in the community. Whether church planting or any other ministry, when people work in areas of their giftedness they are more contented in ministry.

Unexpectedly, it was found that these pastors spend large amounts of focused time with leaders providing practical training to prepare them for church planting. The teaching and training model is (1) from experience, (2) from what the leader is learning, and (3) from practical ministry. Much of it is hands-on training. One church has workers lead a cell group to help them develop a burden for church reproduction. One pastor insists on always doing ministry with others, and many workers learn from the leader's example. One pastor takes members with him to evangelize, but he has the members share their testimonies rather than sharing his own. To provide or support this preparation, several churches have their own in-house "Bible schools" or are closely connected to a local seminary for training while in ministry. These reproducing leaders shared in very clear steps a biblical selection and confirmation process for raising new leaders in the Japanese context. This is done practically by giving them a chance to teach, placing them in ministry and observing them—in one case for up to two years—then confirmation by the church.

The desire is to develop leaders who share the same burden for church reproduction. The pastor wins converts, builds disciples, and raises up leaders. As a mobilizer of people to start new churches, the leader's ultimate role is sending out workers.

Entrust Ministry to Others

These primary leaders receive ministry visions from God and, like themselves, they consequently also encourage their members to receive God's vision for their personal ministry. One example was a secondary leader who was encouraged by her pastor to catch God's plan for her, listen to God's voice, and develop her ministry by being sensitive to the needs around her.

To give members freedom and trust them to work interdependently requires great risk-taking faith by the primary leaders. This was an unexpected research discovery. From the beginning, enjoying an open relationship of trust between the leaders and the believers is crucial in order to confidently delegate service. One pastor explains, "Even though they do ministries freely, they thoroughly talk it through with the [directors], and ministries are handed over based on trust."

In order to entrust ministry properly, leaders must share the desired expectations and philosophy before starting. Several secondary leaders explained that this "setting the table" was extremely helpful in becoming totally responsible for a work. These leaders skillfully entrust responsibility to others and insist on freedom of action for the sake of the ministry. One lay leader related, "Pastor said, then go ahead and try it. And he gave me the responsibility and gave me the freedom. He entrusts us with it." Leaders are not to restrict others, short of retaining the ultimate responsibility when there is a failure. These leaders also provide support for those they have entrusted. A reproducing pastor describes, they "provide them with necessary help for them to carry out the ministries because the members cannot do the ministries without being helped." In many cases, this involves coaching, advising, or going and helping them. This process of being truly entrusted led one secondary leader to say, "We need more leaders like this."

The entire entrusting process is to develop teamwork in mobilization. One lay leader expounded her personal case study:

> I feel that my relationship with the pastor has changed a lot. . . . It was about five years ago when I started to do the ministry God called me to do . . . and we started to work together. Before that, I tried to do what the pastor told me to do. There used to be a string attached to me, as the helper of the pastor. I used to move when the pastor pulled the string up. Then one time I cut the string. I want to do what God tells me to do.

Summary

Lay people are mobilized for ministry by sharing and nurturing ownership of a church reproduction vision. They are selected based on their calling, giftedness, and practical experience and are then prepared through practical hands-on training and eventually entrusted with ministry. According to one pastor, "Disciples are born, raised up, and sent out in this great work. They are sent out to many places including the workplace." He insists the pursuit of developing people and entrusting them with ministry is strategic to growing and reproducing churches, saying,

> If a person wants to multiply churches [as the leader of the church] he needs to actually do it and also develop people. [He needs] to develop people who can be responsible for church planting. I think this is the key for everything. *If the person does not think about planting churches, he will put the people he developed under him and make them his subordinates. Then church planting does not happen.* It is important to develop people for the sake of church planting and send them out. Unless we keep developing people, church multiplication will not occur (emphasis mine).

To reproduce and train lay people, a leader's role must be adjusted radically from a normally traditional approach.

RELATIONAL LEADERSHIP THROUGH ENCOURAGEMENT

Church planting and reproduction cannot be done without a team of people who each require a lot of support, so these leaders focus on encouraging their team members. Their authority in these relationships allows them to release others into ministry, which generates more relational structuring of their churches.

Overall, their priority is people and they are extraordinarily patient with those they lead. In our practice of leadership, we can learn much from these reproducing leaders.

Employ an Encouraging Role

Though they list their primary ministry roles as relational, several leaders made clear they did not see their primary role as pastoral care of people. Pastoral care is implied in any ministry of encouragement; however, the emphasis of encouragement reflects the goal of the leader's role. Are people merely cared for or are people ultimately mobilized for pastoral care?

These church-reproducing leaders choose ministry roles which build relationships and encourage. When asked what they see as their principal roles every primary leader responded with more relational than organizational roles. They listed training, discipling, or teaching, and for them teaching is less lecture and more relational life-on-life training. Other role responses were encouraging and supporting, coaching and mentoring, equipping, and motivating.

As a great example of how to support and encourage other leaders, one pastor has promoted regular retreats for church planters. He also regularly visits them and even invited the interviewer to accompany him. He is excited about the important role of supporting and encouraging people, especially church planters. He asserted, "They don't need our lectures; they need inspiration and encouragement."

Exercise Relational Authority

These reproducing church leaders lead principally by means of their relational authority to appropriately maximize personnel resources. Authority for ministry can come from four sources: position, expertise, relationships, and spiritual authority. These leaders do not lead primarily by means of their positional authority as pastors. These leaders have many effective ministry skills, but they do not rely heavily on the authority of expertise. They exercise authority chiefly through relationships. Their relational authority is interrelated with a ministry of relational encouragement where people are important.

Many have observed tendencies toward a "totally pastor-centered" (Dyer 2013, 97) and lone autocratic leadership style that remains common in Japan (Mullins 1998, 180). This autocratic leadership pattern, prone to a lack of delegation, hinders the growth and reproduction of churches (see chapter two). Leadership that exercises relational and spiritual authority to empower ministry to others was found to be the most effective for growing churches in Japan (Mullins 1998, 180).

Church leadership is both relational and task-oriented. These leaders, in spite of their ministry success, are surprisingly not primarily task-oriented. One leader explained, "It is about people. People are central. Programs are not central."

The agent of securing relational authority is the personal behavior and character of these leaders. When asked what makes a good church leader in Japan, one pastor responded that leadership is "acquired by love . . . Through respecting and trusting others we will also receive trust and respect." The leader's relationship with others is the basis of encouragement in ministry. Another pastor reflected that some pastoral leaders because of limited life experience with people develop inferiority complexes due to the difficulties in building this relational authority.

Releasing Others for Ministry

Both the primary and the secondary leaders prefer a leadership style that allows freedom for lay people to minister. These entrusted leaders are released without restrictions or limitations to fulfill God's vision for their ministries (Eph 4:11–13).

As revealed in this research, two interrelated Japanese leadership issues of authority and control can restrict believers' ministry. First is an extreme authority issue where the leader comes between

God and the believer. This direct obedience to the leader is viewed as oppressive; thus, restricting ministry. One reproducing church pastor defined strong leadership as, "the leader who tells people 'follow me' or 'you follow Jesus by following me.'" Another pastor shared that this "obey me" style of strong leadership is an old style of authoritarian leadership that was once appreciated but is no longer effective. Second is the problem of authority through excessive management and supervision, which restricts freedom and stifles ministry. Removal of this overbearing authority releases people for further ministry, which these leaders endeavor to facilitate.

One church leader revealed that working with his current pastor was different from his experiences with a stricter previous leader who demanded reports and became harsh when things were not going well. He felt this previous leader was a controlling leader. Another secondary leader disclosed that "[the pastor] never controlled me, he would leave it up to me to make my own decisions based on my options."

In an interview one reproducing pastor affirmed, "Never control the person who does the new ministry. Give him 'full independence' and encourage him. . . . Do not control . . . Give encouragement and give blessing [to them]." Another pastor believes using his authority to control people through excessive management in the past caused problems and constricted the believers' freedom. In practice leaders do not tell other workers what they can or cannot do. Leaders can advise them and can discuss matters with them. Similar to parents raising children, leaders cannot live other's lives for them.

How leaders release their people for ministry is not just an issue of encouraging relationships but also an issue of whether overall ministry is progressing. Rather than controlling people, releasing people for ministry actually develops more production capacity for church reproduction. But releasing people also means risk-taking faith in God. Entire movements—not solely individuals—can be restricted, according to a pastor. "If you control, it will die, the fire of church planting will be lost, and the multiplication will be stopped."

Structure Ministry Relationally

Reproducing church leaders encourage relationships in the church by utilizing structures that are more relational and less formal or organizational. This follows from a church philosophy seeing the church primarily as an organism and the people of God rather than simply an organization. While Japanese society continues to have vertical organization and relationships (see Figure 11), these leaders, through relational leadership, have lowered the vertical leadership pyramid and made it less hierarchical, thus making it both flatter and wider (see Figure 12). As he believes all pastors are on an equal level, one leader refuses to use the term assistant or associate pastor, and he personally will not use the term senior pastor. He also has lay people serving as "staff" at the church. One leader is an actual member of a cell group and is accountable to that cell group leader. These examples of flattening the leadership pyramid are a function of authority based less on position and more on relationships. These leaders preferred a leadership role of coordinating and coaching as a means of being less top-down and more alongside.

Several relational metaphors can describe the authority structure in the church. Since one person cannot do church reproduction alone, the church is viewed as a team with the leader as the team captain. Another metaphor used for relations in the church is family. The father who is personal and caring, as well as the head, employs authority. One pastor saw himself as the leader of a church structured like a family. One church leader stated that his pastor's spiritual role in the church was a "spiritual father." In the case of both of these metaphors, the relationship structure is less hierarchical and more like spiritual fathers than like top-down bosses. They are more like "first among equals."

Highly Vertical with a Narrow Base
Enhances differences between types of leaders

Hard Walls
Not very open to leadership expansion

Figure 11. Organizationally-based Leadership Structure

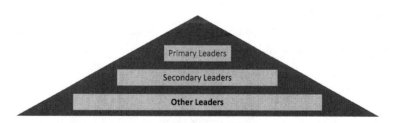

Less Vertical with a Wide Base
Minimizes differences between types of leaders

ThinWalls
More open to leadership expansion

Figure 12. Relationally-based Leadership Structure

Relational encouragement for other leaders comes through the benevolent leadership and the more personal and relational structures of the church.

Applying Relational Patience

Personal relationships are laden with difficulties, and in Japanese society human relationships are even more complicated due to group dynamics. Patience is important in relationships and is one spiritual instrument the leader deploys in relationships. Experiencing patience is incredibly encouraging for people in ministry. These reproducing church leaders are examples of great patience with people and dealing fairly with interpersonal problems.

When asked what makes a good reproducing leader, one pastor disclosed that it is patience that goes beyond words. Patience is important in selecting leaders, and through patience and encouragement people can be moved to situations more suited for them. While only one pastor divulged he had a patient personality, several secondary leaders shared their view that their pastors were patient. In describing the leader's personality, one church leader mentioned that "he is profoundly patient. . . . For example, he does not judge people. He is patient with others, as he believes God can use anyone." Another church leader remarked, "People are not written off just because they have one fault. Some have great gifts but with one fault, it is difficult. But a place is found for them to work, we receive their ministry, we find a place for them. We do not say you have a fault and you cannot serve." He reaffirmed his view of this leader by exclaiming, "His patience is very strong!"

Summary

One reproducing leader articulated that in helping fulfill the vision, his role is to support, encourage, and be patient. Mobilizing members for ministry necessitates that people need to be entrusted, given freedom, supported, and encouraged to continue in team ministry. Leadership must exercise concern for their ministry role, the exercise of authority, and the influences of the structures of the church. All of these point to the necessity of relational encouragement. Another pastor said that his role "is to encourage supervisors and leaders. That means to share together with them about the vision and the purpose given from God." Leadership of reproducing churches is very task intensive but the leader must also be personally encouraging.

AGGRESSIVE IMPLEMENTATION THROUGH PRACTICAL MINISTRY

These church reproducing leaders decisively lead their ministry teams. They are concerned for real-world fulfillment and obedience to the Great Commission. Their role as a leader is to see the church expand and reproduce as a living growing organism. These leaders exhibit three aspects of doing ministry that are insightful and helpful for us. They all implement ministry aggressively, achieve ministry objectives practically and realistically, and lead the church into new directions.

Implement Aggressively

To fulfill a God-given vision, these leaders engage ministry aggressively. They measure success by obedience to scripture. As the church is on the offense and not defense, they are determined to see lay people mobilized in ministry and living out the vital life of the church. They are burdened with the implementation of the vision, not merely thinking or talking about it. When one pastor was asked for practical advice on starting new churches he simply replied, "Just do it. Please do it." These leaders are not passive or indecisive in concrete execution, but are serious about ministry accomplishment. These reproducing leaders are action-oriented. One secondary leader portrayed his pastor simply as "effectual."

These courageous leaders in risk-taking faith do not let obstacles stand in their way. One leader said of his pastor, "He does not give up, has strong tenacity, and continues engaging." They are not afraid of experimenting with new approaches to overcome hindrances to church reproduction. Courageous leadership also means change. One reproducing pastor completely revolutionized his church from a traditional ministry. Another church discontinued a significant, but expensive, ministry because it was not working to accomplish their purposes in the community. This type of leadership means possible failure and even the expectation of failure. Similarly, as they exhibit uncommon patience with people, they also exhibit tenacity with achieving objectives. Misumi's study of Japanese leadership has found that goal-oriented leadership is a very positive trait, especially when the leader couples it with caring for the team (Misumi 1985).

Achieve Practically and Realistically

Leaders of reproducing churches model obedience to God's vision in realistic and practical ways. They put to use the tools of flexibility and creativity to achieve these ministry goals. These leaders are not interested in theory alone but real-world results. According to these leaders, this characteristic is not so much a matter of personality but of ministry behavior. As practical doers their behavior emphasizes doing, not just knowing. When asked for reasons why other churches cannot reproduce, one pastor replied that leaders have not been taught how to do it practically. In contrast, these leaders are incredibly realistic. One example is a pastor who gave advice to those interested in starting churches: "Just do it and find out. I do not believe that if you do this, then this will happen. You do not know until you do it. I am a realist." Practicality is used to overcome obstacles and remove unproductive efforts. This characteristic is the basis for their hands-on training for lay mobilization.

To these leaders, being practical implies being flexible. A church leader revealed, "I feel that the pastor is more flexible than the board members. . . . He is quite flexible." Having a church that is dynamic with a simple relational structure allows easy midcourse corrections. Flexibility allows appropriate changes to surmount obstacles. One pastor suggested including strategies in your original plan to overcome barriers so when you confront them, you can clear these hindrances. According to one church leader who said, "I think he is flexible, because he carefully thinks about what are the current needs without sticking to old [patterns]." Several secondary leaders report that their pastors are not afraid to change and to be relevant for new generations. Studies of church planters in Japan have proven that flexibility is essential, and those that are more flexible with ministry plans are more effective (JEA 1988; KDK 1998).

Being practical also means being creative. Though creativity can lead to being radical, creativity is a characteristic not normally praised in Japanese leadership (Chan et al 1996, 9–10). None of these effectual leaders mentioned that they had the personality trait of creativity, but they mentioned behaving in this way. These leaders find creative ways of applying ministry in different settings. New ideas and attractive ways of ministry are introduced. Several pastors purposely use innovative technology like DVDs and video streaming to overcome the difficulties of distance between churches. They seem to utilize anything in the cause of starting new churches.

Lead into New Directions

These church reproducing leaders accomplish ministry in new areas by using flexibility and creativity. They take courageous initiative to see the realization of the end goal. They are entrepreneurial; like their church planters, they like to start things. Four leaders started the church they now serve, and one leader transformed his church from a traditional model.

They boldly lead in new directions rather than defending or protecting what already exists. A reproducing church cannot be content with protecting the status quo. These leaders do not believe stability to be the true nature of the church and ministry.

A reproducing pastor asserted, "The church is always wanting stability but it cannot reproduce without instability." Moreover, leaders must do what is necessary and, for aggressive leaders, their direction is not toward security or stability because that would undercut risk.

Being this kind of leader means they lead rather than manage what already exists, they do not protect the present situation, and they do not plan routine details. By leading in new directions, these leaders place less importance on management. Leaders who primarily lead rather than manage is a mark of growing churches (Wagner 1984, 44–63). They fulfill their role best by leading others with their gifts and abilities to administer many ministry responsibilities. They coordinate people in ministry, which, inspired by faith, does not undermine personal initiative or creativity.

These reproducing leaders coordinate the big perspective rather than organize or plan routine details, which was somewhat unexpected. Due to the nature of the church being dynamic and alive, they believe no person can control or manage the church. Therefore, detailed planning prevents the leader, as one said, from "go[ing] with [the] flow." Their planning and strategy is practical, based on vision, so as to overcome obstacles. Leadership structure and decision-making are kept simple. In terms of planning skills and gifts, these leaders run the spectrum. One leader is skillful, using others' input to develop plans and to avoid problems. Another leader is not a detailed person and hates details, while yet another pastor revealed he is "not a strategist. I am not the man with the skill, technique. I do not think in an organized way." Conversely, several of the secondary leaders were clearly skilled managers and took care of the managing function for the primary leader.

Summary

These reproducing leaders are people of action. They know about reality and they confront it. They overcome; they do not worry or fret about obstacles and barriers because they expect them to be there. Because they are aggressive implementers, these leaders achieve goals in the real world by being flexible and creative. They do not talk about doing it; they do it. Being realistic and down-to-earth, they have found ways to do it. They indeed start new things, leading in new directions rather than getting involved in routine details of ministry, thus protecting what already exists. Through this determined focus, they see their visions for the church fulfilled through church reproduction.

CONCLUSION

We have seen the six distinctive characteristics for leaders of reproducing churches. These six characteristics are more like an interactive cluster where they all work in concert. In some sense, these characteristics are more about the leaders' vision, faith, and view of the church than other aspects of leadership. Their vision, faith, and theology appear to be a predominant factor and thus affect leadership behavior. In order to fulfill their vision for their image of the church, they feel compelled to practically train people and send them out. This practical application seems to define their personal ministry role, style, and behavior. The final step of sending others would be unlikely without this change in foundational leadership. To view it another way, their practical leadership of reproducing churches derives from their applied theology of the church. A change in leadership role or behavior without the corresponding foundational changes of the view of the church will not result in the same effects in church reproduction.

These leadership characteristics should be viewed as a whole cluster rather than individually. Some may argue that the key characteristic is the major function of developing lay people for church reproduction. However, that function cannot be accomplished without the vital foundation of vision, faith, and view of the church. Once it has been decided people are to be developed, they must be supported with relationships of encouragement and practical implementation.

There are several implications and applications for any leaders and their ministry in the church in Japan. What can be learned from the church leadership of this unique breed of reproducing churches?

First, these leaders and their churches can bring hope to the church. Reproducing churches in Japan are not just theoretically possible, nor are reproducing churches a potential future trend, but reproducing churches are a current reality. This is a reason for hope in Japan! These "best practices" have already happened and are continuing. Also, it is encouraging that leaders reproducing these churches are indigenous, so leadership for church reproduction has happened in the Japanese context and is planted in Japanese soil.

Second is a concern for theological foundations, especially their view of what a church is and who is a leader. These reproducing leaders reported they had a transformed view of the church that affected their vision and faith. This perspective also affected how and why they develop leaders. Their ecclesiology explains their key relational application of church authority and ministry implementation. The implications of foundational theological understandings of the place of lay people in ministry, also the proper ministry role and style for leaders, are extremely timely and important. Misapplied, these are two areas that can considerably hinder the growth of the church. The implications begin with theology since "leadership is intimately related to one's philosophy of life, theology of the church, and understanding of contemporary culture" (Callahan 1997, 38). Leadership begins with applying theology in this manner in the Japanese context.

Third, attention to these leadership characteristics must be used in developing other leaders and assuring progress in church reproduction. The expectation is that these leadership characteristics will be helpful in selecting, recruiting, and mentoring potential church multiplication leaders.

Fourth, all believers must focus on the reproduction of the church. The church in Japan desperately needs to change to become a reproducing church. These leaders challenged the church to a renewed commitment to the priority of evangelism and church reproduction. Just as essential theological principles must lead to practical strategy, to these reproducing leaders, mere words are not enough—the Great Commission demands all of our active obedience.

We have considered strategy, models, and leadership for multiplying churches. In the final chapter, we will consider the opportunities, major issues, and future dreams for planting multiplying churches in Japanese soil.

7

FUTURE CHALLENGES FOR MULTIPLYING NEW CHURCHES

Now to him who is able to do immeasurably more than all we ask or imagine, according to his power that is at work within us, to him be glory in the church and in Christ Jesus throughout all generations, for ever and ever! Amen. Eph 3:20–21

This book was about multiplying new churches in Japanese soil. We considered the soil of Japan, the existing church of Japan, and aspects of church growth and movements in Japan. We also considered a few questions. Why do we need movements of churches in Japan? And why is now the time to consider Japan with greater commitment?

This book is not a how-to manual on how to plant churches in Japan or how to start a church movement. Plenty of other resources are readily available for that purpose.[8] The purpose of the book was to give an update on the possibilities and opportunities for church planting multiplication in Japan. We wish we could offer all the answers to multiplying churches in Japan but that would be unrealistic. Certainly, there is enough material here to challenge all of us as we review and contemplate how to apply various principles for multiplying churches in Japanese soil. We hope it will lead to lots of interaction and discussion.

---

8. The Japan Church Planting Institute has church planting manuals in English and Japanese. JCGI Network has their guidebook for church planting through networks in Japanese with some English helps. There are a few books in print, and other resources are continually being developed.

Hopefully, you will be inspired to pray for more creativity and a larger vision of what it is possible to do in Japan at this time.

Our desire is to see more churches planted, but not just more churches; rather, we want to see the launching of movements of churches that multiply even more churches. Many who work in Japan will have to become "movement pioneers" (Addison 2015) to see this fulfilled.

What should be done to complete the task of reaching the Japanese with a church in every neighborhood? This view of the future means meeting opportunities, considering major issues and questions, and dreaming dreams together.

MEETING OPPORTUNITIES

Especially in recent history, there have been great opportunities for the gospel in Japan. Currently in Japan, there is increased openness due to recent social upheavals and major national disasters. But will these opportunities be lost because of doubt and discouragement?

The opinion of some people toward Christian ministry in Japan is often marked by myths, many of them self-validating. How does our personal theology converge with the reality of Japan? One veteran missionary asserted that in his long career of over forty-five years Japan was unresponsive. In fact, the response in Japan is slow but it is not totally unresponsive. Some Japanese have responded, and Japan is actually full of opportunities. Japan is not closed to the gospel. Japan is very open to religious change as evidenced by the interest in *shin shūkyō* and the *shin shinshūkyō*. Others comment that Japan is closed to the gospel, but surveys reveal people are interested, maybe more open than ever. Japanese are a very dynamic religious people (Stark 2015, 135). Over 30 percent of Japanese are interested in Christianity, and as high as 14 percent of university students report they would like to become a Christian (Gallup 2001). Could doubt have significant influence in preventing some from doing evangelism and so maximizing these opportunities?

Conrad, a veteran Japan missionary, nearly twenty years ago insisted that while several obstacles to church growth in Japan remain, they can be overcome; however, these challenges of the soil of Japan are too often "reinforced by a *fictitious understanding* rather than a true understanding of the situation" (Conrad 1998, 123, emphasis mine). As seen throughout this book from both surveys and ministry experience, the situation in Japan has much better opportunity and the Japanese are far more responsive now than they were twenty years ago. The task of multiplying churches needs to be met with risk-taking faith and clear focus in ministry.

Though the church is declining in some areas, opportunities are also there for growing and reproducing the church. When field research on reproducing churches was released, many in Japan were in denial that reproducing churches existed in Japan. Some believed in the truth of reproducing churches but only for churches in the US. Could it be that many lost their sense of opportunity? Some decry the health of the church in Japan, and there are many places where change is needed (chapter two). Is church health really possible? Though some believe it may be too difficult, opportunities are present in the Japanese culture, as evidenced by the examples of churches modeling the health we are all working toward. The Japanese culture is in fact not out of reach as we have seen that there are some churches reaching whole families and population segments. Can the culture be penetrated? Is Japanese soil responsive to the gospel and fertile for growing the church?

Like the parable of the sower (Matt 13:1–23), in many Japanese hearts their soil is hard, and the devil is busy snatching the truth of the gospel from them. We have also seen that there is rocky soil in Japan where trouble and persecution means people fall away. Furthermore, there are places in Japan where the thorny soil of materialism and group conformity chokes out the fruitfulness of the gospel work. But in Japan there are also places where the soil is good and there is growth and multiplication—thirty, sixty, and a hundred times. Thinking in general terms, Japan is often viewed as not responsive to the gospel. But as we have seen there have been times and places where Japanese have responded to the gospel, planted seeds, and multiplied the church. These opportunities are often hard to anticipate.

The lesson is self-evident; we must sow the gospel more abundantly in Japan. Many have commented on how little the gospel is proclaimed to non-believers. More gospel sowing must occur as the priority of the Great Commission is being witnesses (Acts 1:8) by proclaiming to all what Jesus has done for us (Luke 24:46–48).

The gospel must be sown more skillfully. As we consider the soil of Japan, we are called to expertly communicate the gospel in the Japanese context without compromising the essence of the gospel. The promises of the gospel need to be mastered in order to bring those precious truths to the longing hearts of the Japanese. We need to become experts of the seed as well as specialists in soil science. As sowers of the gospel, we must incarnate and indigenize ourselves along with our message to build trust with the hearers. All of us must become better communicators of the grace of the gospel.

Until God cultivates or replaces the hard soil of Japan completely, we still have opportunities to sow the seed, and continuing faithfulness in unity will prepare for the coming harvest. Tasks as "fellow workers" will be fulfilled by planting the seed and watering it, waiting for God to make it grow (1 Cor 3:5–7). Things are indeed ready; now is the time for work. These are not just responsibilities but God-given opportunities. What is our role in sowing the seed of the gospel? How are we preparing others in the sowing for the harvest? Are we skilled gardeners in God's harvest field?

MAJOR ISSUES AND QUESTIONS

Throughout the book we considered the past history of Japan, the society and the church in Japan, and some contemporary trends. Japan has many cultural, social, and spiritual challenges. Our purpose was to understand the opportunities, potential, and possibilities to thrive in ministry, to combat the status quo, and to strive ahead with new approaches. Throughout the previous chapters, many common themes repeated themselves and raised various questions. There certainly could be many other themes, but these eight are suggested as the major issues to consider.

1. Evangelization and Propagation
We are to "go . . . make disciples" (Matt 28:18). Many are not going and sharing the gospel with others. The focus of our commission is making disciples and not anything else. All growing movements place emphasis on getting the message out to others. How much abundant gospel sowing is going on? How can we encourage more believers to share their faith with others?

2. Leaders' Role as Equipper
Simply "equip the saints for ministry" (Eph 4:12). This theme was clearly seen with Nikolai and the leaders who were reproducing churches. The role of leadership is not solely to protect the flock but to lead them by encouragement and empowerment. Coaching them could be one possible tool. How many people are we equipping to equip others?

3. Mobilize the Laity
In "every spiritual awakening in Christian history [there] has been in some fashion a rediscovery of this revolutionary characteristic" (Sweet 2000, 9). Reproducing churches, growing denominations, and even cults and new religions mobilize the laity for ministry. Practical training for lay people in evangelism, discipleship, and leadership is desperately needed. What percent of church people

are already mobilized in ministry? How do we work at mobilizing all for mission?

4. Grow in Small Groups

Japan is a high relational and collective culture. Growing movements have multiple small groups for relationships, pastoral care, evangelism, and discipleship. Smaller churches, like house churches, are much easier to start. Like the two wings of a bird, small groups can be effective with cell churches when they combine the features of a smaller community and a larger celebration. How are we encouraging small group ministry and supporting them?

5. Aim for Movements of Multiplication

We are to strive for movements of multiplying churches. Movements are possible and we can learn how to foster them. Church size is not important because all sizes are needed, and all types of churches are needed. How can we spur leaders and members to develop movement thinking?

6. Engage the Culture

The church must contextualize the gospel for Japan so it may develop more indigenous forms that will easily reproduce in Japanese soil. How can each part of the church contribute toward becoming "all things to all people" (1 Cor 9:22) so that hearers will grasp the gospel on their terms and be saved? Part of the reason for the rise of the VIP clubs is the timely way they have met the needs of business people whose relationships with the *kaisha* (company) were greatly changed in the turbulent business situation in the 1990s. How can we address spiritual, social, and other needs of Japanese? How can we reach whole families?

7. Renewal of the Church

Where the church exists, a renewal of the church as the body of Christ and its missionary nature of sending is needed. What can be learned from the many healthy reproducing churches? What is the best way to bring about the renewal of the church?

8. Launch Movements of Prayer

All spiritual movements had movements of prayer. How do we encourage prayer movements for the people and nation of Japan that can lead to a missiological breakthrough? We are to "Ask the Lord of the harvest, therefore, to send out workers into his harvest field" (Matt 9:38). How much do we actually pray for the nation of Japan?

God is working in these eight themes, and God will work again. We should seek more opportunities to work together with believers from other groups for common goals and purposes. By networking and partnering together we can raise vision for more churches and develop shared training and support systems for those churches and planters.

One example of applying these themes is Pastor Yukikazu Otomo of the Shiogama Bible Baptist Church. He received a vision from God and then developed a strategy mobilizing and equipping the laity to utilize the house church model in a network covering his entire Miyagi prefecture. He developed this strategy as a doctoral student completing the strategy in January 2011 (Otomo 2011). The triple disaster happened a few months later, and since then he has applied these principles to seeing the vision being fulfilled in the growing Miyagi Mission Network.

While we may bemoan the slow response, we must remove hindrances and stop doing what is preventing evangelism and church reproduction. Ineffective models based solely on tradition need to be discarded for the growth of the church. As seen in this book, when the church moves away from attractional models of evangelism and clergy-centered leadership, the church grows. We must struggle against the status quo that does not seem committed to abundant gospel sowing, leaders as equippers, and using laity in significant ministry. What is preventing these from occurring? How can we eliminate these hindrances and obstacles?

Some affirm that the reason for the slow response in Japan is periods of persecution and restraint by the Japanese government (Lienemann-Perrin 2015). This would be historically true for the "Christian Century" and the decline in Christianity due to systematic persecution. This could also explain some of the challenges in the Meiji era. However, this argument does not work in the environment of religious freedom for the past seventy post-war years. Today there are some valid concerns for a possibly resurgent nationalism or government changes to religious freedom laws, both of which could potentially impinge on evangelism and church planting. We cannot let fear of persecution or these doubts deter us from moving ahead with God's agenda in Japan.

God will bring movements of multiplication. That is his desire. The culture and society of Japan cannot resist his kingship. Movements can happen. "With man this is impossible, but not with God; all things are possible with God" (Mark 10:27). It must happen for the sake of God's glory in Japan. What are God's next steps for you?

We are talking about many changes in the church and how those who believe in Christ are to live and carry out ministry. Some things will continue to be great challenges. To begin we must undergo new thinking and paradigm shifts. We will have to abandon some well-loved traditions.

One example is a Japanese pastor whose church was over fifty years old and only had six members, four of them women. He heard about an effective multiplying house church movement with his denomination in another country. To learn about this ministry, he went on a short mission trip. Within two years of his return, he has started fifteen house churches each with between 6–12 members. What an amazing change in results. This pastor had undergone change along with his church.

But change can scare people. In his case, other pastors have expressed dislike of his ministry because they feel he is rejecting essential church tradition. Will he continue to honor God by these changes or will he compromise to keep in favor with his pastoral group? Many will have to learn to swim upstream against common patterns from other churches and leaders. We continue in the spiritual battle against Satan and his opposition to the gospel and the church. In some cases, we may meet opposition within the Japanese culture itself. We must be prepared to follow God faithfully as his disciples. Effective leaders speak up by setting direction and thus becoming change agents (Nanus 1992, 12–14; see Kouzes and Posner 1995).

DREAMS AND VISION

To achieve what we desire for multiplying churches, we will need many new dreams and visions. Fighting against the status quo or "business as usual" will disturb the well-protected harmony in Japan. In this process we should expect opposition and barriers from every direction.

To see the development of church multiplication, there are some perspectives and directions that need to come to an end, and there are other things which must be started anew. These changes will realign the priorities, calendars, and budgets of many people.

We should expect some opposition from long-standing leaders as the established church is declining and demanding more resources. Because of a wish to preserve some struggling churches, there is a concern that very few seminarians would be available for planting new churches. A professor from one of the largest seminaries in Japan recently recounted that when current students were asked if they were interested in church planting, not one indicated interest. With demands for young pastors to replace those that are retiring, a lack of grand vision for church planting throughout Japan, formal theological training focused on preserving "parish ministry," and a sense to preserve church institutions, we only expect people touched with a unique vision from God to move into church planting.

We need to radically invert the concern, energy, and focus of the church in Japan. In the parable of the lost sheep, when the shepherd realizes that one sheep out of one hundred is missing he goes, finds the one, and rejoices as he returns with the lost sheep (Luke 4:4–7). This is a parable teaching about the vast love God has for each of us and his desire that we be found. There are 99 percent safe and 1 percent lost. God cares for the 1 percent.

In the church in Japan, this parable could be told nearly in the reverse. About 1 percent know Jesus and are safe with the Christian flock while 99 percent are lost. Many Japanese churches have turned inward, focused on this Christian flock, and have merely a 1 percent vision. They are primarily concerned with protecting the sheep and preserving the church while there are 99 percent of the Japanese who are still lost. We all with bold risk-taking faith, without neglecting those in the fold, should develop a 99 percent vision and focus on working with those who are outside the fold.

We are asking for many to have a dream for the 99 percent. How will they hear the gospel from the lips of a Japanese person? How will the resultant believers be gathered into groups of Christians? How will they grow and lead to develop more churches for more people? How could the Christian population grow to 2, 5, or 10 percent? Is your vision only for the 1 percent, or for the 99 percent still needing the gospel?

> Someone in the church must paint the dream. For anything to happen there must be a dream. And for anything great to happen there must be a great dream. The growing edge church will be a painter of great dreams for all of its people, something to lift their sights above the ordinary and give them a great goal to strive for—something for each person to strive for. (Greenleaf 2002, 101)

For a growing group of Japanese leaders, they are beginning to dream of a church for every Japanese. Momentum seems to be growing for church planting and multiplying movements throughout the entire country in Japan. Many of these visionary leaders gathered at the first Church Multiplication Vision Festa in October 2014 with sixty-five participants. In October 2015, their numbers exploded to 180. Over 150 leaders gathered during the Sixth Japan Congress on Evangelism in September 2016 and agreed to keep dreaming together. Ninety leaders met in Tohoku for the 2017 Vision Festa. We hope the momentum for the dream will continue to grow towards the Seventh Congress on Evangelism in 2023.

This book has shown in broad strokes that what occurred in Japan's past could again become reality. Infectious evangelism going from one natural relationship to another. People curious about the faith and coming to Christ. Leaders and pastors gathering these new believers together for worship and prayer, then discipling them and sending them out to evangelize more.

In discussions about reaching all of Japan by saturating each community with churches, some equate the number of churches required to the number of local post office banks serving residents throughout Japan. Others have considered the number of over fifty thousand convenience stores positioned where every Japanese can be served in their community. Global missiologists use a practical guideline of one church for every 2,500 people. In view of the current population, Japan would need at minimum of fifty thousand churches. "Fifty thousand" has emerged several times but should not be considered a "magic number." But "50,000 churches" is serving as a rule of thumb for the dream toward a national church multiplication initiative moving forward. This initiative would be a broad-based evangelical movement for an ongoing focus of our energies toward the goal of Japan saturated with churches.

Although Japan needs fifty thousand churches, and it must be done, with current human resources this task appears extremely difficult. The need for fifty thousand church planters raises many practical problems, not to mention the thousands of coaches and trainers it would entail to prepare and support them. But others, like the beginnings of Holiness Church, faced very similar challenges and met them with bold, risk-taking faith and creative innovation. Furthermore, they fostered a vision that would sustain them not just to meet their goals but often to pass their set goals.

In the Philippines in the early 1970s, there were only a small number of about eight thousand evangelical churches. At that time, several leaders from a cross-section of major evangelical groups dreamed of planting a church in every neighborhood and village in their country. They networked together for vision, prayer, training, coaching, research, mobilization, and leadership so that every neighborhood would be evangelized and have a church established. These leaders strived together as strategic partners in evangelizing, discipling, and training for church planting. This DAWN vision of a goal of fifty thousand churches was realized and exceeded before their twenty-year target date. In a similar vein, through the Global Church Planting Network (GCPN), other leaders from many nations are discussing these types of national initiatives for church planting in East Asia including Taiwan, Mongolia, South Korea, and Japan.

There are some leaders in Japan who are beginning to dream these dreams. What would be a God-honoring national goal for church planting? How could we in faith achieve it? What would we need to see it fulfilled? Like these visionary leaders, we need to take our eyes off of the weaknesses of the church at this point and see the potential for multiplication movements. In chapter four we looked at some trends and networks. Today there is encouraging news of the convergence of several streams of networks and ministries interested in church planting movements. All these groups involved are cooperating and networking with the Church Multiplication Vision Festa.

Until a national initiative develops, we must be faithful to our calling, maximize our opportunities, and go through any open door. For us, now is the time of opportunity. While fostering local and regional vision, we should mobilize everyone for impact and maximize whatever you can wherever you are. One Japanese pastor in a large city has done a bit of dreaming. He knows that his city of seven churches really needs one hundred churches to be saturated, so he started four more churches and is currently targeting a neighboring village. He is working with other churches and networking to see more.

To see these dreams fulfilled we will need to bring more clarity to the task before us in Japan. This raises for us several key questions. How do we return to the basics and hone down church ministry to the essential core that is not necessarily based on buildings or programs or even clergy? How do we reach the Japanese people? What model churches and examples will we learn from? Where are the churches that are innovative and effective, and that humbly want to become ministry learning centers for others?

CONCLUSION

There are many opportunities, numerous issues to practically address, and dreams and visions from God to fulfill. The Japanese are the second largest unreached people group in the world. Whether you are a pastor, a lay worker, or a missionary, this will demand consecrated prayers, wise research, and many pioneer church planting initiatives to saturate the nation with communities of God's people.

We took a look back at the history of the church and what has worked. We took a look inward at the church and what is needed to change. We took a look outward and considered the culture and society of Japan. Most of all, we need to take a look upward to God in dependence and faith. Japan is in a spiritual battle preventing the preaching of the gospel (Eph 6:19–20), blinding the minds of unbelievers (2 Cor 4:4), and thus hardening the soil of their hearts, along with confusing and misdirecting the church through evil schemes (Eph 6:11). This demands we stand and put on the armor of God. All of our spiritual warfare is to be coupled with the power of prayer. This work is not by our human cleverness, diligence, or skill but rests on the spiritual power of God. We must cultivate hearts of repentance and faith to depend more on him to work our visions and ministries.

This is not a book fascinated with numbers for church growth. Rather, it is for the glory of God that we work to deliver the Japanese from darkness and see the transformation of individuals and society. We need to see anew that multiplying churches in Japanese soil is God's desire. Our vision is for Japan to be filled with communities of worshippers of the one true God. We want to see God's reign and rule over every nook and cranny of Japan as the kingdom of God comes. We see the vision for his church—the people of God—joined in great unity, loving each other, fellowshipping together as community, and serving the world in word and deed. We want to see the power of the gospel transform our lives, our communities and churches, the nation of Japan, and indeed the entire world. This is all in the mind of our glorious God, as God is a sending God.

We must also take a look ahead to the future. I have not tried to predict what God might do or not do in Japan. I am confident in his promises to his people and his church. Adoniram Judson, the early Baptist missionary to Burma, which at that time was considered very hard soil, had a great word of encouragement: "The prospects are as bright as the promises of God." We need to rest on God and what he wants and only he can do. "'Not by might nor by power, but by my Spirit,' says the Lord Almighty" (Zech 4:6). May God's mercy for Japan be great, his gospel run through the nation, and his Spirit quicken many who would be a part of a great throng no one could count through multiplying churches in Japanese soil.

In the days, months, and years ahead, what will you do to further multiply churches in Japanese soil?

REFERENCES

Addison, Steve. 2015. *Pioneering Movements: Leadership That Multiplies Disciples and Churches.* Downers Grove, IL: Intervarsity Press.

Akae, Hiroyuki. 1997. "Kyōkai Kaitaku [Church Pioneering]." In *Fukuin ni Tsutaeru Kyōkai* [A Church Propagating the Gospel], 106–12. Tokyo: Word of Life Press.

Allison, Gregg. 2012. *Sojourners and Strangers: The Doctrine of the Church. Foundations of Evangelical Theology.* Wheaton, IL: Crossway.

Anderson, Allan Heaton. 2013. *An Introduction to Pentecostalism.* 2nd edition. New York, NY: Cambridge University Press.

Barna, George, ed. 1997. "The Vision Thing." In *Leaders on Leadership*, 47–60. Ventura, CA: Regal Books.

Beilby, James K. and Paul Rhodes Eddy, eds. 2012. *Understanding Spiritual Warfare: Four Views.* Grand Rapids, MI: Baker Academic.

Bosch, David J. 1991. *Transforming Mission: Paradigm Shifts in Theology of Mission.* Maryknoll, NY: Orbis Books.

Braun, Neil. 1971. *Laity Mobilized: Reflections on Church Growth in Japan and Other Lands.* Grand Rapids, MI: Eerdmans.

Bryant, David. 1995. *The Hope at Hand: National and World Revival for the Twenty-First Century.* Grand Rapids, MI: Baker Books.

Callahan, Kennon L. 1997. *Effective Church Leadership: Building on the Twelve Keys.* San Francisco, CA: Jossey-Bass Publishers.

Chan, Darius K. S., Michele J. Gelfand, Harry Triandis, and Oliver Tzeng. 1996. "Tightness-looseness Revisited: Some Preliminary Analyses in Japan and the United States." *International Journal of Psychology* 31:1–12.

Chizuo, Shibata. 1985. "Some Problematic Aspects of Japanese Ancestor Worship." In Bong Rin Ro, ed. *Christian Alternatives to Ancestor Practices*, edited by Bong Rin Ro, 247–60. Taichung, Taiwan: Asia Theological Association.

Christian Shimbun. 2016. "Japan Mission Map." *Christian Shimbun*, March 30, special supplement.

Church Information Service (CIS). 2013. "The Protestant Church in Japan in 2012." *Church Information Service News* 75 (December): 4–5.

Conn, Harvey. 1984. *Eternal Word and Changing Worlds.* Phillipsburg, NJ: P & R Publishing.

Conrad, Stan. 1998. "Encountering Japanese Resistance." In *Reaching the Resistant: Barriers and Bridges for Mission*, edited by J. Dudley Woodberry, 117–31. EMS 6. Pasadena, CA: William Carey Library.

Cozens, Simon. 2010. *Leadership in Japanese House Churches.* Gloucester, UK: Wide Margin Books.

Dale, Kenneth J. 1975. *Circle of Harmony: A Case Study in Popular Buddhism with Implications for Christian Mission.* Pasadena, CA: William Carey Library.

———. 1996. *Coping with Culture: The Current Struggle of the Japanese Church.* Lutheran Booklets, No. 3. Tokyo: Lutheran Booklet Press.

———. 1998. "Why the Slow Growth of the Japanese Church?" *Missiology: An International Review* 17: 275–88.

Drummond, Richard Henry. 1971. *A History of Christianity in Japan.* Grand Rapids, MI: Wm. B. Eerdmans Publishing Co.

Dyer, Stanley R. 2013. *Communication in Community.* Bellville, ON: Guardian Books.

Earhart, H. Byron. 2004. *Japanese Religion: Unity and Diversity.* Fourth Edition. Boston, MA: Wadsworth.

———. 2014. *Religion in Japan: Unity and Diversity.* 5th edition. Boston, MA: Wadsworth.

Ellwood, Robert. 2008. *Introducing Japanese Religion.* New York, NY: Routledge.

Eriyakai [Elijah Group]. 2009. *Eriya no you ni: Watashi wa kawaru, anatamo kawaru, nihon ga kawaru* [Like Elijah: I will change, you will change, Japan will change]. Eriyakai shuppan iinkai [Elijah Group Publication Committee]: Tokyo.

Fleming, Dean. 2005. *Contextualization in the New Testament: Patterns for Theology and Mission.* Downers Grove, IL: Intervarsity Press.

Foxwell-Barajas, Alanna. 2012. "Second Chances in Japan: One Year after Disaster, Sacrificial Giving Gains Churches New Credibility." *Christianity Today* 56 (3): 15–17.

Fujino, Gary. 2007. "The House/Cell Church for Mission in Today's Japan." *Japan Harvest* 58 (4): 2–3.

———. 2009. "House, Cells and Church Planting Movements in Japan Today." *Japan Harvest* 61 (1): 23–24.

Fujisawa, Chikao. 1958. *Concrete Universality of the Japanese Way of Thinking: A New Interpretation of Shintoism.* Tokyo: The Hokuseido Press.

Fukuda, Mitsuo. 1993. *Developing a Contextualized Church: As a Bridge to Christianity in Japan.* Gloucester, UK: Wide Margin Books.

———. 2000. "A Case Study of the International VIP Club: A Mission Movement Among Japanese Businessmen." In *Strategies for Christian Witness in a Postmodern World,* edited by Russell Sawatsky and Cynthia Dufty, 90–97. The Forty-first Hayama Missionary Seminar: Amagi Sanso, Japan.

————. 2001. "Sermon Topics Contextualized for Japan." *Journal of Asian Mission* 3 (1): 141–48.

————. 2002. "Nihon ni okeru kaitaku dendō ni tsuite: Hesselugrabu hakase e no intabyu [Regarding Church Planting in Japan: An Interview with Dr. Hesselgrave]." In. *Senkyōgaku ridingusu Nihon bunka to kirisutokyō [Readings in Missiology: Japanese Culture and Christianity]*, edited by Mitsuo Fukuda, 172–78. Hyogo Ken, Japan: RAC nettowaku [RAC network].

————. 2015. "Toward a New Breed of Churches in Japan." In *Becoming the People of God: Creating Christ-centered Communities in Buddhist Asia*, edited by Paul H. de Neui. Seanet Volume 11. Pasadena, CA: William Carey Library.

Furuya, Yasuo, ed. trans. 1997. *A History of Japanese Theology*. Grand Rapids, MI: Eerdmans.

————. 2006. *History of Japan and Christianity*. Ageo-shi, Saitama: Seigakuin University Press.

Gallup Organization. 2001. *Changes in a Changing World: Final Report*. Prepared for Aim International by Gallup Japan. April 10, 2001. Unpublished Report.

Garon, Sheldon M. 1986. "State and Religion in Imperial Japan, 1912–1945." *Journal of Japanese Studies* 12 (2): 273–302.

Garrison, David V. 2004. *Church Planting Movements: How God is Redeeming a Lost World*. Midlothian, VA: WIGTake Resources.

Gibbs, Eddie. 2005. *Leadership Next: Changing Leaders in a Changing Culture*. Downers Grove, IL: InterVarsity Press.

Global Church Advancement. 2007. *GCA Church Planter Basic Training Manual*. Altamonte Springs, FL.

Goto, Makito. 2011. *Nihon Senkyō-ron [Missiology in Japan]*. Tokyo: E-grape.

Greenleaf, Robert K. 2002. *Servant Leadership: A Journey into the Nature of Legitimate Power and Greatness.* Mahwah, NJ: Paulist Press.

Guthrie, Stan. 1995. "Mavericks in Japan Bucking for Change." *World Pulse* 30 (11): 1.

Hardacre, Helen. 1986. *Kurozumikyo and the New Religions of Japan.* Princeton, NJ: Princeton University Press.

Hari, Yoshiya. 2017. "Rising from the Rubble: How God Used Disaster to Raise Up a New Leadership Generation." In *Eastern Voices: Volume 1: Insight, Perspective, and Vision from Kingdom Leaders in Asia In Their Own Words,* 37–60. Cerritos, CA: Asian Access.

Helms, Marilyn M. 2003. "Japanese Managers: Their Candid Views on Entrepreneurship." *Competitiveness Review* 13 (1): 24–34.

Hesselgrave, David J. 1978a. "Nichiren Shōshū Soka Gakkai: The Lotus Blossoms in Modern Japan." In *Dynamic Religious Movements: Case Studies of Rapidly Growing Religious Movements around the World,* edited by David J. Hesselgrave, 129–48. Grand Rapids, MI: Baker Book House.

———. 1978b. "What Causes Religious Movements to Grow?" In *Dynamic Religious Movements: Case Studies of Rapidly Growing Religious Movements Around the World,* edited by David J. Hesselgrave, 297–326. Grand Rapids, MI: Baker Book House.

———. 2005. *Paradigms in Conflict: 10 Key Questions in Christian Missions Today.* Grand Rapids, MI: Kregel Publications.

Hiebert, Paul G. 1982. "The Flaw of the Excluded Middle." *Missiology: An International Review 10.* (January 1982), 35–47.

Hiebert, Laurence D. 2012. "Employing Varied Japanese Cultural Forms to Illustrate Biblical Truths." D.Min. major project, Trinity International University.

Hofstede, Geert. 1984. *Culture's Consequences: International Differences in Work-related Values.* Abridged ed. Vol. 5, Cross-cultural Research and Methodology series. Newbury Park, CA: Sage Publications.

———. 1997. *Cultures and Organizations: Software of the Mind.* New York, NY: McGraw Hill.

House, Robert J., Paul J. Hanges, Mansour Javidan, Peter W. Dorfman, and Vipin Gupta, eds. 2004. *Culture, Leadership, and Organizations: The GLOBE Study of 62 Societies.* Thousand Oaks, CA: Sage Publications.

Hori, Ichiro. 1968. *Folk Religion in Japan: Continuity and Change.* Chicago: Univ. of Chicago Press.

———, ed. 1972. *Japanese Religion: A Survey by the Agency for Cultural Affairs.* Tokyo: Kodansha International Ltd.

Hymes, David. 2016. "Toward a History and Theology of Japanese Pentecostalism." In *Global Renewal Christianity; Spirit-Empowered Movements: Past, Present, and Future.* Vol. 1 Asia and Oceana, edited by Vinson Synan and Amos Yong, 158–78. Lake Mary, FL: Charisma House.

Ikegami, Yoshimasa. 2003. "Holiness, Pentecostal, and Charismatic Movements in Modern Japan." In *Handbook on Christianity in Japan*, 125–42. Handbook of Oriental Studies, Section Five, Japan, edited by Mark R. Mullins. Boston: Brill.

Ikubo, Zoe. 2015. *JCMN Coaching Network Summary Report.* Unpublished paper.

Izuta, Akira. 1998. "Ookina Kyōkai Dewanaku Ooku no Kyōkai [Not Toward Bigger Churches but Toward More Churches]" In *Kaitaku Dendōsha e no Okurimono [A Present to Church Planters]*, 7–13. Tokyo: Kokunai Dendou Kai (KDK) [National Evangelism Association].

Jacobsen, Morris. 1977. *Japanese Church Growth Patterns in the 1970s.* Tokyo: Japan Evangelical Missionary Association.

JCE6 (Japan Sixth Congress on Evangelism). 2016. *Databook: A Look at Japan Mission in the Future.* Tokyo: Word of Life Press.

Japan Mission Research (JMR). 2015. *JMR Chosa Reporto 2014 Nen [Japan Mission Research Survey Report 2014]*. Inzai City, Chiba Japan: Tokyo Christian University.

JEA Church Planting Survey Committee. 1988. *Church Planting Survey: Interim Report. JEA Consultation on Evangelism.* Karuizawa, Japan. September 1988. Japan Evangelical Association.

Jennings, J. Nelson. 2003. "Theology in Japan." In *Handbook on Christianity in Japan*, 181–203. Handbook of Oriental Studies, Section Five, Japan, edited by Mark R. Mullins. Boston: Brill.

———. 2008. "Paul in Japan: A Fresh Reading of Romans and Galatians." In *Power and Identity in the Global Church: Six Contemporary Cases*, edited by Brian M. Howell and Edwin Zehner. Pasadena, CA: William Carey Library.

Joshua Project. 2015. "Unreached Listings: 100 Largest Unreached Peoples." Accessed June 15, 2015. http:// joshuaproject.net/listings/Population/desc/100/allctry /allcon/allreg?jps2=5&jps3=5#list.

Kawasaki, Hiroshi. 2002. "Church Multiplication through Networking." In *Japan Evangelism*. 2002 CPI Conference Special ed. 1:45–47.

Keller, Timothy J. 2012. *Center Church: Doing Balanced Gospel-Centered Ministry in Your City*. Grand Rapids, MI: Zondervan.

Kharin, Iiya. 2014. *After Nicolas: Self-realization of the Japanese Orthodox Church, 1912–1956*. Gloucester, UK: Wide Margin.

Kishida, Kaoru. 1992. "Nihon no Senkyō Senryaku ni Tsuite [Concerning Japan Mission Strategy]." In *Nihon, Ajia Soshite Sekai e [Japan, Asia then to the World]*, 43–48. Tokyo: Third Japan Congress on Evangelism Publications Committee.

Kokunai Dendou Kai (KDK). 1986. "1986 Survey of Kokunai Dendou Kai (KDK) Pastors: Summary of Responses having Potential Significance." Unpublished manuscript.

———. 1998. *Kaitaku Dendōsha e no Okurimono [A Present to Church Planters]*. Tokyo: Kokunai Dendou Kai (KDK) [National Evangelism Association].

Kouzes, James M. and Barry Z. Posner. 1995. *The Leadership Challenge: How to Keep Getting Extraordinary Things Done in Organizations*. San Francisco, CA: Jossey-Bass Publishers.

Lausanne Movement. 1993. "Statement on Spiritual Warfare." http://www.lausanne.org/content/statement/statement -on-spiritual-warfare-1993. Accessed June 25, 2015.

Lee, Robert. 1967. *Stranger in the Land: A Study of the Church in Japan*. World Studies of Churches in Mission. London: Lutterworth Press.

———, ed. 1995. *The Japanese Emperor System: The Inescapable Missiological Issue*. Tokyo: Tokyo Mission Research Institute.

———. 1999. *The Clash of Civilizations: An Intrusive Gospel in Japanese Civilization*. Harrisburg, PA: Trinity Press International.

Lewis, David C. 2013. *The Unseen Face of Japan*. 2nd ed. Gloucester, UK: Wide Margin.

Lienemann-Perrin, Christine. 2015. "Christian Mission in Japan's History: Failure of Success?" *Princeton Theological Review* 18 (1) Accessed June 13, 2016 http://ptr.sga.ptsem.edu.

Macfarlane, Alan. 2007. *Japan through the Looking Glass*. London: Profile Books.

Matsumoto, David. 2002. *The New Japan: Debunking Seven Cultural Stereotypes*. Yarmouth, ME: Intercultural Press.

Matsunaga, Kikuo. 1999. "Theological Education in Japan." In *Preparing for Witness in Context: 1998 Cook Theological Seminar*, edited by Jean S. Stoner, 295–311. Louisville: Presbyterian Publishing House.

McFarland, H. Neill. 1967. *The Rush Hour of the Gods: A Study of New Religious Movements in Japan*. New York, NY: Macmillan Co.

McQuilkin, Robertson. 2007. *The Five Smooth Stones: Essential Principles for Biblical Ministry*. Nashville, TN: B & H Publishing.

Mehn, John W. 2007. "Perspective on Church Models." *Japan Harvest* 58 (4): 10–11.

———. 2010. "Characteristics of Leaders Reproducing Churches in Japan." D.Min. major project, Trinity International University.

———. 2013. "Leaders Reproducing Churches: Research from Japan." In *Missionary Methods: Research, Reflections, and Realities*, edited by Craig Ott and J. D. Payne. EMS 21. Pasadena, CA: William Carey Library.

———. 2014. "Apostles to Japan: Ralph Cox and Joseph Meeko." *Japan Harvest* 65 (4): 24–26.

Misumi, Jyuji. 1985. *The Behavioral Science of Leadership. An Interdisciplinary Japanese Research Program*, edited by M. F. Peterson. English ed. Ann Arbor, MI: University of Michigan Press.

Mitani, Yasuto. 2007. "The Church Should React to Needs and Change from an Inward Focus to an Outward Focus." *CIS News* 69, 9. September 2007.

Mitsumori, Haruo. 2002. "The Church in the First Year of the 21st Century." *Church Information Service News* 55: 6.

Miyamoto, Ken Christoph. 2008. "Worship is Nothing but Mission: A Reflection on Some New Opportunities." In *Mission in the Twenty-First Century: Exploring the Five Marks of Global Mission*, edited by Andrew Walls and Cathy Ross, 157–64. Maryknoll, NY: Orbis Books.

Miyazaki, Kentaro. 2003. "The Kakure Kirishitan Tradition." In *Handbook on Christianity in Japan*, 19–34. Handbook of Oriental Studies, Section Five, Japan, edited Mark R. Mullins. Boston: Brill.

Montgomery, Jim. 1997. *Then the End Will Come*. Pasadena, CA: William Carey Library.

Moore, Ralph. 2009. *How to Multiply Your Church: The Most Effective Way to Grow*. Ventura, CA: Regal Books.

Moreau, A. Scott. 2005. "Contextualization." In *The Changing Face of World Missions*, edited by Michael Pocock, Gailyn Van Rheenen and Douglas McConnell, 321–48. Grand Rapids: Baker Academic.

Mullins, Mark R. 1990. "Japanese Pentecostalism and the World of the Dead: A Study of Cultural Adaptation in Iesu no Mitama Kyōkai." *Japanese Journal of Religious Studies*. 17 (4): 353–74.

———. 1992. "Japan's New Age and Neo-New Religions: Sociological Implications." In *Perspectives on the New Age*, edited by James R. Lewis and J. Gordon Melton, 232–46. Albany, NT: SUNY Press.

———. 1998. *Christianity Made in Japan: A Study of Indigenous Movements*. Honolulu, HI: University of Hawai'i Press.

———. 2003. "Indigenous Christian Movements." In *Handbook on Christianity in Japan*, 143–62. Handbook of Oriental Studies, Section Five, Japan, edited by Mark R. Mullins. Boston: Brill.

———. 2006. "Japanese Christianity." In *Nanzan Guide to Japanese Religions*, edited by Paul Loren Swanson and Clark Chilson, 115–28. Honolulu, HI: University of Hawaii Press.

Murray, Stuart. 2001. *Church Planting: Laying Foundations*. North American ed. Scottdale, PA: Herald Press.

Naganawa, Mitsuo. 2003. "Archbishop Nikolai Kasatin: A Russian Evangelist in Japan." In *Saint Nikolai Kasatkin and the Orthodox Mission in Japan*, edited by Michael Van Remortel and Peter Chang, 122–38. San Francisco, CA: Divine Ascent Press.

Nagasawa, Makito. 2002. "Religious Truth: From a Cultural Perspective in the Japanese Context." *Journal of Asian Mission* 4 (1): 43–62.

Nanus, Burt. 1992. *Visionary Leadership: Creating a Compelling Sense of Direction for Your Organization.* San Francisco, CA: Jossey-Bass Publishers.

Nethercott, Paul. 2007. "Jesus LifeHouse—Part Two." *Japan Harvest.* 58 (3): 12–14.

O'Brien, P. T. 1995. *Gospel and Mission in the Writings of Paul: An Exegetical and Theological Analysis.* Grand Rapids, MI: Baker Books.

OC International Japan. 1993. *Establishing the Church in Japan for the Twenty-First Century: A Study of 18 Growing Japanese Churches.* Kiyose City, Tokyo: OC International Japan.

Ohashi, Hideo. 2007. *Kyōkai seichō dokuhon [Church Growth by the Book].* Tokyo: Inochi no Kotobasha [Word of Life Press].

Otomo, Yukikazu. 2011. *Miyagi ken nai no kyōkai zōshoku no Teigen: Shinto Shutai no "Ie no Kyōkai" ni yoru kaitaku dendō. [A Proposal for Church Multiplication in Miyagi Japan: A Laity—Based House Church Model].* D.Min. major project, Luther Rice University.

Otomo, Yukikazu. 2016. *Higashi nihon daishinsai to kyōkai zōshoku [Great East Japan Disaster and Church Multiplication].* Tokyo: Asian Access Japan.

Otomo, Yukikazu, Hatsuo Shibata, and Eriko Houlette, eds. 2016. *Shisai to shinkō chōsa: Hokokusho [Disaster and Faith Survey: Report Book].* Tokyo: Japan Mission Research.

Ott, Craig. 2015. "Globalization and Contextualization: Reframing the Task of Contextualization in the Twenty-first Century." *Missiology: An International Review* 43 (1): 43–58.

Ott, Craig and Steven J. Strauss. 2010. *Encountering Theology of Mission: Biblical Foundations, Historical Development, and Contemporary Issues.* Grand Rapids, MI: Baker Academic.

Ott, Craig and Gene Wilson. 2011. *Global Church Planting: Biblical Principles and Best Practices for Multiplication.* Grand Rapids, MI: Baker Academic.

Okawa, Shuhei. 2002. *Seishoteki ridashippu to nihon bunka [Biblical Leadership and Japanese Culture].* Tokyo: Malkoushu Publications.

Parrish, Scott. 2008. "The State of the Kingdom of God in Japan: An Analysis of the Church Information Service 2007 Annual Report." *Japan Harvest* 60 (1): 17–22.

Payne, Jervis David. 2009. *Discovering Church Planting: An Introduction to the Whats, Whys, and Hows of Global Church Planting.* Colorado Springs, CO: Paternoster.

Pease, Richard Bruce. 1989. "Japanese Leadership Styles: A Study in Contextualizing Leadership Theory for Church Growth in Japan." Th.M. thesis., Fuller Theological Seminary.

Peters, George. 1981. *A Theology of Church Growth.* Grand Rapids: Zondervan.

Piper, John. 2010. *Let the Nations be Glad: The Supremacy of God in Missions.* 3rd ed. Grand Rapids, MI: Baker Academic.

Prohl, Inken. 2012. "New Religions in Japan: Adaptations and Transformations in Contemporary Society." In *The Handbook of Contemporary Japanese Religion,* edited by Inken Prohl and John K. Nelson, 241–67. Leiden: Nederlands.

Reader, Ian and George J. Tanabe Jr. 1998. *Practically Religious: Worldly Benefits and the Common Religion of Japan.* Honolulu: University of Hawaii Press.

Reid, David. 1991. *New Wine: The Cultural Shaping of Japanese Christianity.* Berkeley, CA: Asian Humanities Press.

Reischauer, Edwin O. 1988 *The Japanese Today: Change and Continuity.* London: The Belknap Press of Harvard University Press.

Research F Group. 2012. *Nihon dewa naze fukuin senkyō ga mi o musubanakatta ka* [Why has gospel mission not borne any fruit in Japan?]. Tokyo: Word of Life Press.

Robinson, Haddon. 1999. "Foreword." In *Developing a Vision for Ministry in the 21st Century*, by Aubrey Malphurs. Grand Rapids, MI: Baker Books.

Robinson, Martin, and Stuart Christine. 1992. *Planting Tomorrow's Churches Today: A Comprehensive Handbook*. Kent, UK: Monarch Publications.

Satake, Tokio. 1994. "A Successful Church Planter." In *The Harvester's Handbook: Evangelism and Church Planting in Japan*, edited by Japan Evangelical Missionary Association, 40–42. Tokyo: Japan Evangelical Missionary Association.

Schwarz, Christian A. 1996. *Natural Church Development: A Guide to Eight Essential Qualities of Healthy Churches*. St. Charles, IL: ChurchSmart Resources.

Sherrill, Michael John. 2002. "Church Vitality in Japan." PhD diss., Fuller Theological Seminary.

Shimazono, Susumu. 1986. "Conversion Stories and Their Popularization in Japan's New Religions." *Japanese Journal of Religious Studies*. Religion and Society in Contemporary Japan. 13 (2/3): 157–75.

———. 2003. "New Religions and Christianity." In *Handbook on Christianity in Japan*, 277–94. Handbook of Oriental Studies, Section Five, Japan, edited by Mark R. Mullins. Boston: Brill.

Solheim, Dafinn. 1986. "Church Planting in Japan Since 1945." In *Church Planting Patterns in Japan*. The Twenty-Seventh Hayama Men's Missionary Seminar: Amagi Sanso, Japan, edited by Carl C. Beck, 7–19.

Stamoolis, James J. 1984. "Eastern Orthodox Mission Theology." *IMBR* 8 (3): 59–63.

————. 1986. *Eastern Orthodox Mission Theology Today*. American Society of Missiology series, no 10. Maryknoll, NY: Orbis Books.

Stark, Rodney. 2015. *The Triumph of Faith: Why the World is More Religious than Ever*. Wilmington, DE: ISI Books.

Stetzer, Ed. 2012. "Paul and Church Planting." In *Paul's Missionary Methods*, edited by Robert L. Plummer and John Mark Terry. Downers Grove, IL: Intervarsity Press.

Stetzer, Ed and David Im. 2016. *Planting Missional Churches: Your Guide to Starting Churches that Multiply*. 2nd edition. Nashville, TN: B&H Academic.

Sugimoto, Yoshio. 2014. *An Introduction to Japanese Society*. 4th ed. Cambridge University Press.

Sweet, Leonard. 2000. "Foreword." In *Equipping the Saints: Mobilizing Laity for Ministry*, edited by Michael J. Christensen and Carl E. Savage. Nashville, TN: Abingdon Press.

Toyotome, Masumi. 1985. "To Reach Japan Smaller is Better." *Evangelical Missions Quarterly* 21 (3): 230–37.

Trevor, Hugh. 1993. *Japan's Post-war Protestant Churches*. Unpublished paper.

Tsukii, Hiroshi. 2002. "Toward a Lay-led Evangelism and Pastoring Church Planting Strategy: Our Sojourn in Developing Cell Groups at Hongodai Christ Church." In *Japan Evangelism*. 2002 CPI Conference Special ed. 1:48–49.

Wagner, C. Peter. 1984. *Leading Your Church to Growth*. Ventura, CA: Regal Books.

————. 1990. *Church Planting for a Greater Harvest: A Comprehensive Guide*. Ventura, CA: Regal Books.

Wan, Enoch and Elton S. L. Law. 2014. *The 2011 Triple Disaster in Japan and the Diaspora: Lessons Learned and Ways Forward*. Portland, OR: Institute of Diaspora Studies.

Winter, Ralph D. 1997. "Three Types of Ministry." *Evangelical Missions Quarterly* 33 (4): 420–22.

———. 2002. "From Mission to Evangelism to Mission." *International Journal of Frontier Missiology.* 19 (4): 6–8.

Winter, Ralph D., and Bruce A. Koch. 1999. "Finishing the Task: The Unreached Peoples Challenge." In *Perspectives on the World Christian Movement: A Reader,* edited by Ralph D. Winter and Steven Hawthorne, 509–24. 3rd ed. South Pasadena, CA: William Carey Library.

Wong, Ben. 2010. "Coaching by Focusing on the Essence." *You Can Coach: How to Help Leaders Build Healthy Churches through Coaching, edited by* Joe Comiskey, Sam Scaggs, and Ben Wong, 107–28. Moreno Valley, CA: CCS Publishing.

Yamamori, Tetsunao. 1974. *Church Growth in Japan: A Study in the Development of Eight Denominations 1959–1939.* South Pasadena, CA: William Carey Library.

Yoshimoto, Hiroko, Simon Cozens, Mitsuo Fukuda, Yuji Hara, Atsuko Tateishi, Ken Kanakogi, and Toru Watanabe. 2016. "A Post-3/11 Paradigm for Mission in Japan." *International Journal of Frontier Missiology.* 33 (1):17–21.

Zielenziger, Michael. 2006. *Shutting Out the Sun: How Japan Created Its Own Lost Generation.* New York, NY: Doubleday.

Other books available from

WILLIAM CAREY
LIBRARY

www.missionbooks.org
1-866-730-5068

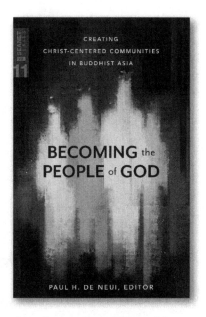

Becoming the People of God
Creating Christ-centered Communities in Buddhist Asia (SEANET 11)

Edited by Paul H. De Neui

~~List Price: 17.99~~

Our Price: 14.39

How do Christ followers celebrate unity in the midst of diversity? How do we become the people of God in more than name only? A unifying Christ-centeredness demands living out kingdom values and bearing witness to transformation in and through a multitude of cultural manifestations. We struggle to serve, worship, and witness in the midst of this age-old challenge.

Christ followers are in the process of becoming what will one day culminate in a huge and startling celebration of people from all of God's beloved creation. If you are interested in hearing from those discovering what that might look like outside traditional packaging, this book is for you.

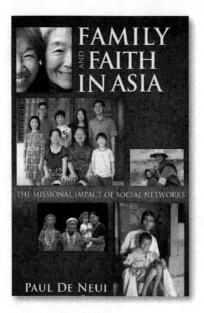

Faith and Family in Asia
The Missional Impact of Social Networks (SEANET 7)

Edited by Paul H. De Neui

~~List Price: 19.99~~
Our Price: 15.99

If Christian mission in Asia and most of the non-Western world is
ever to advance, it must seriously consider the importance of family
networks. Far too long the strategy of a "one by one" approach
has stifled the spread of the gospel, reinforced a highly individu-
alized unbiblical theology and destroyed social relationships that
might lead to conversation, conversion, and social transformation.
Family and Faith in Asia: The Missional Impact of Extended Networks
attempts to issue a wake-up call to serious reflection on a highly
ignored social reality in Buddhist and many other social contexts.
The book is a resource useful for anyone wishing to study practical
approaches to issues related to family and faith in Asia, particularly
in Buddhist contexts for mission.

Innovation in World Mission
A Framework for Transformational Thinking about the Future of World Mission

By Derek Seipp
~~List Price: 12.49~~
Our Price: 9.99

Our world is changing: mass migrations, the emergence of mega-cities, globalization, travel, and ubiquitous connectivity. How do we make sense of it all? *Innovation in World Mission* was written for those who care about being relevant in this chaotic, yet exciting new world. This book explores the categories of mega-changes happening around us, and the impacts they are making, specifically in world mission. It explores how God created us in his image, to be creative and innovative—modern day children of Issachar who understand change and know how to respond. Real-life examples from ministries, non-profits, and businesses are used throughout to help understand how to put these tools into practice.

Understanding Insider Movements
Disciples of Jesus within Diverse Religious Communities

Edited by Harley Talman and John Jay Travis
Our Price: 39.95

For the first time in history, large numbers of people from the world's major non-Christian religions are following Jesus as Lord. Surprisingly for many Western Christians, they are choosing to do so within the religious communities of their birth and outside of institutional Christianity. How does this work, and how should we respond to these movements?

The first book to provide a comprehensive survey of the topic of insider movements, *Understanding Insider Movements* is an indispensable companion for those who want to glimpse the creative, unexpected, boundary-crossing ways God is at work among the peoples of the world in their diverse religious communities.